WHEN GOD MADE FOOTPRINTS ON THE EARTH

Volume Two – The Devotional Message of Christmas

Herb Hodges

WHEN GOD MADE FOOTPRINTS ON THE EARTH

Volume Two – The Devotional Message of Christmas

©2012 Herb Hodges

ALL RIGHTS RESERVED

No part of this publication may be reproduced, stored in a retrieval system, or transmitted in any form without prior written permission.

Spiritual Life Ministries
2916 Old Elm Lane
Germantown, TN 38138
Herb Hodges – Executive Director

Web Site: herbhodges.com
E-mail: herbslm@mindspring.com

Table of Contents

Preface - 5

Chapter 1
A COMPLETE CHRISTMAS – 11

Chapter 2
THE DIVINE BULL'S-EYE
OR IT HAPPENED AT BETHLEHEM - 27

Chapter 3
THE MONSTER, THE MAGI,
AND THE MONARCH - 39

Chapter 4
HEAVEN'S MONOGRAM
OR GOD'S STANDARD PROCEDURE - 51

Chapter 5
TOO GOOD TO BE FALSE - 69

Chapter 6
THE FIRST CHRISTMAS GIFTS - 87

Chapter 7
THE SALVATION STORY - 103

PREFACE

When Mary and Joseph were first shocked by the announcement of Heaven's angels that Mary's body would be the vehicle for the Incarnation of the Son of God, one of the things the angel Gabriel said to them about Jesus was this abrupt statement: "He shall be great" (Luke 1:32). Is this not the understatement of the ages? No such short announcement can begin to inform us of the magnitude of His greatness. HIS greatness was completely different from the relative "greatness" of any and every human being.

Historically, Jesus would be greater than any other human being. He was greater *in Person* than any other human being. He was greater in *Purpose* than any other human being. He was greater in *Performance* than any other human being. He was greater in *Product* than any other human being. These sentences are not merely a clever way to arrange and use words. They are the very essence of the greatness of Christ. In order to at least *touch upon* the greatness of His Person, let's place Him in contrast to some of the greatest people who have lived on this earth.

Jesus was greater than *John the Baptist.* Though it was also said of John that "he shall be great," the contrast of John and Jesus will clearly reveal that these are relative terms when used of John and Jesus. Jesus was superlatively greater, supernally greater, eternally greater, than John the Baptist, though Jesus acknowledged John as the greatest of mere men (Luke 7:28). Someone said that Jesus was "as much better than John as eternity is more than time", and "as much greater as Messiah is greater than 'a voice in the wilderness'."

Take a giant step back in history and see our next contrast. Jesus is greater than *Abraham.* The Jewish elders once cynically said to Jesus, "Are you greater than our father Abraham? …. Whom makest thou thyself?" (John 8:53). Jesus forever settled that contrast by answering, "Before Abraham was—indeed, before Abraham came to be—I AM." Why didn't Jesus say, "Before Abraham was, *I was*"? The answer is that, if He had said that, He would be reducing His ascendant Person. Jesus was eternally pre-existent before *all things or beings, and no matter where you locate Him in time or eternity, He is ever and always, "I AM".* Another has wisely said, "Jesus is as much greater than Abraham as Jehovah is greater than Jehovah's 'friend'."

Go forward from Abraham, and note that Jesus is greater than *Jacob.* A sin-stained Samaritan woman asked Jesus, "Are you greater than our father Jacob?" This time, Jesus revealed His greatness by addressing her deepest need and His ability and willingness to meet that need. He said, "If you knew the gift of God, and who it is who said to you, Give me a drink, you would have asked of Him, and He would have given you living water!" (John 4:10). Then He added, "Whoever drinks of this water (the water of Jacob's well, where their conversation took place) shall thirst again, but whoever drinks of the water that I shall give him shall never thirst; but the water that I shall give him *shall be in him a well of water springing up into everlasting life."* Jacob dug a well that provided *earthly* water, but Jesus gives *living water* from God, thus He is conspicuously greater than Jacob.

Move another step forward in history and consider that Jesus is greater than *Solomon.* With a wisdom that was supernatural and never humanly surpassed, Solomon was described in the Bible as being "wiser than all men" (I Kings 4:31). But "Behold, a greater than Solomon is here" (Luke

11:31). "In HIM are hidden all the treasures of wisdom and knowledge" (Colossians 2:3). How much greater is HE than Solomon? Jesus is as much greater than Solomon as the Giver of wisdom is greater than the wisdom He gives.

Jesus is also greater than *Jonah*. This is not at all hard to substantiate, though Jonah's name is a great name of Old Testament history. He alternates in the book that bears his name between prodigal, pray-er, penitent, and pouter. Despite that poor succession in his life, he was still used to bring a million Ninevites to their knees in repentance before God. In our terms, Jonah may have been used of God to lead the greatest "revival" in history. Because he was "swallowed into a place of death," and later was "vomited" out alive on dry land, he provides at least a picture of the Death and Resurrection of Jesus. We are thus reminded through a "prodigal prophet" that Jesus also rose up from among the dead. Ah, but Jesus was "raised after the power of an endless life." He is "alive forevermore". He is Himself "the resurrection and the life" (John 11:25). Unlike Jonah, Jesus did not rise again to mere natural life. At His resurrection, He gained a glorified spiritual body, and is Himself the Resurrection and the Resurrecting One. He was declared to be "the Son of God with power by His resurrection from the dead" (Romans 8:2), and thus there is "no comparison", only contrast, between Jonah and Jesus. Jesus is easily and infinitely "greater than Jonah".

"Jesus was given a more excellent Name than they" — or any accumulation of "theys". I remind you of merely one of the great reasons for His superlative greatness. Jesus is great, greater than all, for the single, simple, eternally significant reason that He meets and solves the only ultimate problem in the universe, the massive problem of *sin*. He saves men finally from Satan, from death, and from Hell, but Satan, death and Hell are problems only because of *sin*. The answer?

The angel declared it to Mary when he said, "You shall call His Name JESUS, for He shall save His people from their sins." Note that He does not save people *in* their sins, but He fully, finally, freely and forever saves His people *from* their sins. And right now, in our "ground zero", the very day in which we are living now, "sin shall not have dominion over us"(Romans 6:14) as we yield ourselves entirely to His Lordship. Thus, "the law of the Spirit of Life in Christ Jesus makes us free from the law of sin and death" (Romans 8:2).

Now, to the subject at hand. Jesus was "greater", also, as to His *origin*. As impossible as it seems to men whose "possibilities" are bound by what we know of time and space, Jesus was not born like any other human being who has ever lived. He was "from above". As staggering as the Truth is, He was Divinely born as a human being, "born of a virgin" — without the biological agency of human fatherhood. Begotten of the Holy Spirit, He is and always will be *"the unique Son of God."* This book which you hold in your hands is a devotional reminder of how His earthly life began; it is a primer on the great Christmas story. Christ became "the Son of Man" that we might become "sons of God." Dear friend, if you do not have a vast vested interest in Him today, I hope you will find such as you read the pages ahead.

A COMPLETE CHRISTMAS

I Timothy 3:16: "And without controversy great is the mystery of godliness: God was manifest in the flesh."

I. A BABY IN A CRIB

II. A MAN ON A CROSS

III. A BODY IN A TOMB

IV. A KING ON A THRONE

Chapter 1

A COMPLETE CHRISTMAS

I Timothy 3:16:

"And without controversy great is the mystery of godliness: God was manifest in the flesh."

The daily newspaper of Sunday, December 21, 1997, carried a magnificent Gospel message in Johnny Hart's "B. C." comic strip. By his personal testimony and the public testimony he incorporates often into his comic strips, it is apparent that Johnny Hart knows Something Awfully Big—in fact, it is evident that he knows it (Him) well! The comic strip was built around this poem:

"It seems to me that since the 'Fall' — without even thinking it odd,

That man has had no trouble at all, Believing that he can be God.

How he would do this I cannot conceive, Tho' he certainly thinks he can;
And yet, he cannot bring himself to believe, *That **God** can become . . . a **man**.*"

Does Johnny Hart know The Story — or what?

Let's "try on" a poetic presentation that may have more theological clout, but not more profundity. This poem was written by an Englishman named H. R. Bramley.

"A babe on the breast of a maiden He lies,
Yet sits with the Father enthroned in the skies;
Their faces from Him the Seraphim hide,
Yet Joseph stands unafraid by His side.
O wonder of wonders, what more can unfold?
The Ancient of Days is but a few hours old;
The Maker of all things is made of the earth;
Man is worshiped by angels, and God comes to birth.
The Word in the bliss of the Godhead remains,
Yet in flesh he suffers the keenest of pains;
He *is* what He *was* and forever *shall be*,
But *became* what He was *not* for you and for me."

One little boy got thoroughly confused as he was reciting the Lord's Prayer in a candlelight Christmas Eve service. When he came to the "trespasses" part, he said, "And forgive us our *Christmases* as we forgive those who *Christmas* against us!" Everywhere we see figures of Santa and his reindeer, striped candy, mistletoe, holly wreaths, and sparkling lights—in most places, we see everything *but* Jesus. We would be wise to pray, "Lord, forgive us for *our kind of Christmas*, and move us again to *Your kind of Christmas!*"

But what *is* God's kind of Christmas? Pastor Stephen Crotts was right when he said, "Christmas was actually a

33-year event." Christian author and educator T. S. Rendall wrote, "In reading a biography we never stop after having read about the birth and early years. We keep on until we have read the entire account of the subject's life." However, many people today celebrate the season and the sentimentality of Christmas and totally disregard "the rest of the story." In the early church, they magnified the rest of the story (the life, death, resurrection, ascension, etc.)—and didn't even celebrate Christmas at all! In fact, the celebration of Christmas apparently did not begin until sometime in the fourth century after Christ. So what is *God's* kind of Christmas? What is this "33-year event"?

I. A BABY IN A CRIB

First, the story of Christmas is the story of *a Baby in a crib.* At Bethlehem, God dropped an anchor squarely in the middle of the mainstream of history. A baby in a crib, and wonder of wonders, the Baby was God! At Bethlehem, He who made man was made man! Here was the greatest case of planned parenthood the world has ever seen! In fact, Jesus was the only person in history who could plan His own birth. But then after an eternity of planning, He was still only born in a barn, in a despised out-of-the-way country. Was it a case of poor planning—or did He know something we don't know? The truth is that God is at home in barns and despised places—provided they will accommodate Him! It is not that He has a prejudice against palaces, but people in palaces usually do not want Him.

The shepherds were only "on their way to Bethlehem" for several hours, and the wise men for several months, but Jesus had been "on the way to Bethlehem" for all eternity! When Adam sinned in the Garden, Jesus had already "packed His bags" for Bethlehem. On that "holy night," when "God reduced Himself to the span of a woman's womb," God came to where we were, that He might finally take us to where He is. The newborn Babe of Bethlehem was the everlasting God come "down from His glory." This Infant "with no language but a cry" was the Eternal Word Who spoke the worlds out of the womb of nothing. The tiny arms of this helpless Child were the limbs of Him who laid the timbers of the universe. In the crib, the Most High became the Most Nigh, the Infinite became the Intimate. In face, the Limitlessly Infinite became the Locally Definite. God built a bridge across the deep, wide chasm of sin and *came to us. He came to us because we could not go to Him.* Why did He come? "To bring us to God" (I Peter 3:18). But before He could bring us to God, another dimension had to be added to the story.

> "Sing lullaby! Hush, do not wake the Infant King.
> *Soon comes the cross, the nails, the piercing.*
> Then in the grave at last repining. Sing lullaby!"

II. A MAN ON A CROSS

Second, the complete Christmas story is the story of *a man on a cross.* A biography doesn't stop with the birth and early life of its subject. In fact, when it's time to honor historical figures who have a day set aside for them on our calendar, we don't think about them as babies. We don't keep pictures of cuddly little Abe Lincoln in the log cabin where he was born in Kentucky. In the story of Jesus, also, we must continue reading until we have finished the entire account. With Jesus, the "rest of the story" is the Best of the story. The Virgin Birth was the first historical step toward the Cross. In fact, one theologian phrased the combination of His Birth and His Death in this graphic sentence: "Theologically and spiritually, it is as if Jesus was born in a tomb." Just as Bethlehem, the place of His Birth, and Jerusalem, the place of His Death, are less than ten miles apart, so His Birth and His Death are very closely connected.

Charles Dickens illustrated the truth of Christ's death for men and their sins when he allowed Sydney Carton to die in the place of Charles Darnay in <u>A Tale of Two Cities</u>. All the sympathy in the world could not have kept Darnay from the guillotine once the revolutionaries had marked him for death. His only way out was through the death of a substitute. Even so, *Christ died as a substitute for sinners!*

When Jesus was born, He came into fallen humanity, cursed by sin, and though He was personally free of both the sin and the curse, He took both the sin and the curse upon Himself, and passed down into death itself. We cannot now properly celebrate Christmas without realizing the Cross in the midst of it all.

Jesus not only came *to* us; He also came *for* us. The word "for" must be translated carefully here. It is a word of *sympathy*—Jesus is *for* me (John 3:18). But it is also a word of *substitution*. Jesus died, "the just *in place of* the unjust, that He might bring us to God" (I Peter 3:18).

This peculiar and poignant story will illustrate the part that Christ's Person and Sacrifice had in covering man's sin. An eight-year-old boy was in class, taking a test. He was so nervous and distraught over the possibility of not completing the test on time and not making a passing grade that he suddenly and uncontrollably wet his pants. He was wearing dark trousers, and he hoped that the evidence of his mishap would not be seen. However, when he looked down at the floor, he saw a telltale puddle beneath his feet. Already sick with panic, he looked up in time to see the teacher moving down the aisle toward him. What could he do? Everybody will see, everybody will laugh, and I will never recover, he thought.

What the boy didn't know was that at that very moment one of his classmates, a little girl who sat behind him in class, was coming up the aisle from behind him, carrying the large goldfish bowl which she had just taken from the classroom window sill. When she got alongside his seat, she suddenly tripped and dropped the heavy bowl. It shattered on the floor with a loud crash and sent water, broken glass, and the fish flying everywhere across the floor. Some of the water even splashed up on the boy's legs. He was rescued! With the evidence of his problem now covered by the water of the fish bowl, the boy experienced a rush of relief (forgive the pun; you could call it a second relief). Thank God! What a wonderful gift! My problem is covered!

But then it dawned on him that boys were not even supposed to like little girls. So he looked at her and sternly said, "What's wrong with you? Can't you hold onto *anything*? Can't you watch where you are going?" The boys laughed at the girl, the boy recovered his dignity, and the teacher took him to the gym to get him some dry clothes to wear.

At lunchtime, no one sat with the little girl. Even her friends avoided her at recess. In the unforgiving society of elementary school, she was suddenly without companions, though she was normally a very popular girl.

When the school day was over and the students were walking away from school, the boy walked out the door and saw the little girl, walking alone toward her home. He thought back over the episode in the classroom that day and suddenly, on an impulse, he walked over to her. He said to her, "You know, I've been thinking of what happened during the test today. What you did wasn't an accident, was it? You did that on purpose, didn't you?"

She answered quietly, "Yes, I did do it on purpose. I knew what . . . what had happened to you. You see, I wet my pants once, too."

What a great Gospel illustration! Every one of us had "wet his pants" in a big, bad way. The stain, and shame, and humiliation of our sin is real, and if it has not yet been fully seen, it will one day be exposed. But Jesus Christ has *covered* for us (the exact meaning of *kaphar*, the Old Testament word for *atonement*)! He shed His blood, He *poured out* His blood for you and for me (the girl did not merely "spill" the water; her act was intentional), with the intent of covering our sins, their stains, and the shame and humiliation of them. He took all of our blame and all of our shame upon Himself. And He fully, finally, freely and forever covered us and our sins. Now I am clean! He saw my hopeless situation and rescued me. He has given me dignity and hope and a brand new start. Hallelujah, what a Savior!

An old Appalachian Gospel folk song says,
"I wonder as I wander out under the sky,
  Why Jesus the Savior came forth to die,
  For poor ornery sinners like you and like I.
  I wonder as I wander out under the sky."

As sinners, we needed more than His company, His example, His sympathy, or His teaching. So "He was delivered over to death for our sins" (Romans 4:25). As a result of His Full Settlement for our sins at Calvary, the holy and just law of God is satisfied, God Himself is propitiated, and I am free to be received into fellowship with my Heavenly Father. What a Gospel! But before it is a full Gospel, still another dimension must be added to the story.

III. A BODY IN A TOMB

Third, the complete Christmas story is the story of *a body in a tomb.* Here again, we are dealing with the solid stuff of history. The resurrection is no illusion produced by wishful people. It stands concretely in the domain of definite objective reality. Anyone with uncertainties should avail himself of one of the great books on the historical occurrence of the resurrection (and there are *many* such books) and see for himself. I have read dozens of such books over the years. I have just read John Ankerberg's book, <u>Knowing the Truth About the Resurrection</u>, which I would highly recommend to any seeker.

In spite of the overwhelming evidence for the resurrection of Christ, human flesh has strained to the limit to try to argue another explanation for the disappearance of the body from the tomb on the morning of the resurrection. One such "explanation" is the "swoon" theory of the resurrection. A story will help us see both the theory and the fallacy of it. A college student had just returned to school from the Easter break. She approached a much-loved Bible professor with this question: "The preacher at the church I attended while I was at home said that on the first Good Friday, Jesus really just swooned on the cross and the disciples revived him and nursed him back to health. What do you think?" The wise professor, tongue in cheek, replied, "Next time you go home, look up that preacher and give him thirty-nine lashes with a cat-o'-nine-tails. After that, make him lie down on a cross and nail him to it. When he is securely fastened, raise the cross with him on it and drop the bottom of its main beam into a deep hole. Leave him hanging out there in the afternoon sun for several hours. Along the way, run a spear through his heart, and when he looks dead, embalm his body and place it in a musty, damp tomb for a couple of days and see what happens!" 'Nuff said about *that* "explanation"! And all the others are equally ridiculous.

There are really only three possibilities in explaining the Empty Tomb. The first possibility is that Jesus' ***foes*** took the body. Even the slightest investigation will show how ridiculous this view is. All that would have been necessary to destroy any possibility of a Christian movement would have been for them to produce the body, but they did not do so because they could not do so. The second possibility is that His ***friends*** took the body. Only an ignorant person would take such a view seriously. Read the story for yourself in the Gospels and then ask the question, "In their demoralized state, and with the maximum security guard that stood at the tomb, *could* they have removed the body?" And if they could have, why *would* they? Most of the Apostles of Jesus were martyred for their faith. Now, men will lie in order to avoid death, but they will not die for a lie. The only other possibility is that His ***Father*** "disposed" of the body by raising Him bodily to life again. Certainly it involves a miracle, but it is even *logically* the only viable and reasonable explanation of what happened. Any open-minded reader of the Gospel accounts, considering all the evidence, would be forced to a positive conclusion about the resurrection of Christ. And *theologically*, it was an absolute necessity. If Jesus' body had remained in the grave, the transaction necessary for our salvation would have remained incomplete. A dead Savior is no Savior. It is the resurrection that shows God's acceptance of Jesus' payment for our sins, and it is the resurrection that demonstrates Him to be the "Son of God with power" (Romans 1:4). He was "raised again for our justification" (Romans 4:25).

Long ago, when the Pharaoh of Egypt exalted Joseph to be next to him on the throne he made him the source of life itself to all the people. No one could even eat without Joseph's permission. In fact, the issue of life and death rested entirely in Joseph's hands. Even so, Jesus is now in full authority over all matters in heaven and on earth (Matthew 28:18). If I want to live spiritually, Jesus is the only Bread of Life. If I ignore Him, I will starve my own soul forever. The destiny of every human being lies in Jesus' sovereign hands. In the old story, Joseph not only saved his brothers from death, he also was the means of their being kept alive and on good terms with Pharaoh. He became their companion and sponsor. Even so, Jesus is with us as our Companion and Sponsor, as His Christmas name, IMMANUEL, tells us (Matthew 1:23). Through His *Death*, He became our *Savior*. Through His *Resurrection*, He became our *Sponsor*. What a Gospel!

IV. A KING ON A THRONE

Finally, the complete Christmas message is the story of *a king on a throne*. After His Death, Jesus was buried, and then He rose again from the dead. Then, He ascended to Heaven and today, He occupies a place of sovereignty at God's right hand. Both at the beginning and the end of His earthly life, Jesus was proclaimed to be a King. "Where is He that is born King of the Jews?" the wise men asked. "This is the King of the Jews," read the inscription which Pilate placed over Jesus' head on the cross. He didn't *look* like a King on either occasion, but those who surrendered to His sovereignty at His Birth and at His Death discovered that He *is* "King of Kings," and that He will share His reign with those who trust Him. In fact, twice during His public ministry, He was offered a crown— once by Satan during the temptation in the wilderness (Matthew 4), and once by the people when they tried to make Him a monarch by force (John 6). However, if His innate royalty became somewhat apparent even in the days of His flesh, when He was subject to the limitations incident to His

Incarnation and when He deliberately hid Himself (*"veiled in flesh* the Godhead see," our Christmas carol says), how much more evident it must have been when, having laid those inhibiting restrictions aside, He ascended into Heaven and sat down on the right hand of the Majesty on high.

When Prince William of England was born on June 21, 1981, the *London Telegraph* published a 32-line ode to the baby. Any American might be able to pray a part of this prayer this Christmas, since we have recently suffered through our own national "day of horror." Simply replace the word "politicians" with the word "terrorists," and replace the word "British" with the word "universal," and you have the Message. *Time* magazine printed the following selected lines from the ode to Prince William on July 5, 1981

> "O God, Who was Thyself a Child,
>   But scorned among Thine own,
>   Who was declared the highest King,
>   But had no earthly throne —
>   Save us from politicians
>   Whose tricks our state would cast down
>   And bless the baby who is born
>   To wear the British crown."

Whether Prince William will ever wear the British crown is still in question, but Jesus was "the Man who was *born* King."

You will pardon another illustration from royal British history. When Queen Elizabeth of England was still a little girl, her royal parents held a party for a large number of British dignitaries at Buckingham Palace. It was their intention to host the party in the gardens of the Palace grounds, but a heavy rainstorm on the day of the party forced a change of plans. The party was moved indoors into a large room of the Palace. During the party, Elizabeth and her younger sister happened into the room where the party was held. They immediately became the center of attention. After awhile, the questions, answers, and polite conversation subsided. At that moment, Elizabeth saw a painting of the crucifixion of Jesus on a wall near where she was standing. She pointed toward the painting and remarked, " My papa says *that's* the man who is *really* king."

One author wrote, "The immense step from the Babe at Bethlehem to the living, reigning, triumphant Lord Jesus, returning to earth for His own people—that is the glorious truth proclaimed throughout Scripture." The return of Christ is a colossal distance from the Bethlehem manger, but it may be mere seconds away from us. The clouds may break at any moment and Christ will reappear. So the Christmas hymn is true, "Bethlehem's manger cradled a King."

Jesus is already on the throne today, waiting for His enemies to be made His footstool (Hebrews 1:13). The One whose head was wreathed in a crown of thorns then is now wearing the diadem of sovereignty and glory. Every day, in a practical way, I prove that without His total reign in my life, I am in total ruin. But what a joy when my daily biography is written as another happy episode of "The King and I"!

He went from the *communion of Heaven* to *a crib in a cattle stall* in Bethlehem. Then He went from the *crib* to the *cross*. Then from the *cross* to the *crypt*. Then from the *crypt* to the *crown*. *Crib, Cross, Crypt, and Crown.* These ingredients, properly mixed, constitute a complete Christmas. I hope you stop to adore Him at each one of these places in the next few days. I hope you celebrate a complete Christmas with Christ at the very heart of the celebration.

Perhaps someone is reading these lines who has never received Christ and trusted Him for salvation from sin and for the gift of eternal life. What must you do? Simply and honestly confess your sins directly to God, the One against Whom you have sinned. Remember that Jesus loves you personally and died personally for You. Remember, too, that He "was raised from the dead for your justification (for your salvation)" (Romans 4:25). Remember, too, that He said that if you would trust Him and receive Him into your heart, He would save you, forgive your sins, give you the gift of eternal life, and live in you all the way to His home in Heaven. I join with the Holy Spirit in urging you to trust Jesus today. If you do, this Christmas will be your *first real* one.

THE DIVINE BULL'S-EYE
or
IT HAPPENED AT BETHLEHEM

Matthew 2:1; Luke 2:15

" . . . *Jesus was born in Bethlehem of Judea in the days of Herod the king* . . ."
" . . . *Let us now go even unto Bethlehem* . . ."

I. A PLACE OF SUFFERING AND SORROW

II. A PLACE OF SHARING

III. A PLACE OF SOVEREIGNTY

IV. A PLACE OF SELF-SACRIFICE

Chapter 2

THE DIVINE BULL'S-EYE
OR
IT HAPPENED AT BETHLEHEM

Matthew 2:1; Luke 2:15

" . . . Jesus was born in Bethlehem of Judea in the days of Herod the king . . ."

" . . . Let us now go even unto Bethlehem . . ."

A Penn State football player (a defensive tackle, probably) was asked, "Where was Jesus born?" "In Lancaster?" he asked tentatively. *"Lancaster*? Of course not!" the questioner exclaimed. "Pittsburgh?" he asked meekly. "You gotta be kidding," the questioner said disgustedly, "Any idiot should know that Jesus was born in Bethlehem." The player said with a shrug, "Well, I knew it was *somewhere in Pennsylvania!"* Most Americans are at least aware that Jesus was born in Bethlehem, though their awareness of the message and the meaning of Christmas often goes no farther than that.

During the Christmas season, the attention of the Christian world — and much of the pagan world – is turned toward the little Palestinian village of Bethlehem. The word "Bethlehem" is a Hebrew word which means "House of Bread." This name perfectly suited the favored little village. It was built on a fertile Palestinian hillside; its fields grazed rich flocks of sheep and goats; its lush valleys were covered with wheat and barley; its terraced slopes with almond and olive, fig and pomegranate, rising to the twin summits above the town. Sheltered among the trees were the famous vineyards that made Bethlehem's wine more choice than Jerusalem's, only five miles away. As far back in the history of the village as the Old Testament book of Ruth, the farmers of Bethlehem had always been men of wealth. In Ruth 2:1, a Bethlehem farmer is described in these words: "And Naomi had a kinsman of her husband's, a mighty man of wealth, and his name was Boaz."

But man does not live by bread alone, nor can he afford to labor only for the meat that perishes. Here, to Bethlehem, in the fulness of time and the hunger of the world, came He who was to be for all men the Bread of Life, taking upon Him, in innocence and beauty, that flesh which He was to give for the life of the world. It was no accident that Jesus was born in Bethlehem. We are all aware that God's providence selected the site for the birth of Jesus, but I am certain that none of us has ever fully realized the preparation of the town for the coming of Christ.

In his famous Christmas hymn, "O Little Town of Bethlehem," Phillips Brooks wrote these words:

"In thy dark streets shineth, The everlasting light;
The hopes and fears of all the years Are met in thee tonight."

Pastor Brooks must have written these words under the impulses of Divine illumination. Everything in man's predicament that needed a treatment was present at Bethlehem! And everything in God's heart that needed an expression was present at Bethlehem! Bethlehem symbolized in its history all the pathos, sadness, and need of the human race; and it brings before the world a tremendous picture of loving self-sacrifice. And all of these can be seen in Bethlehem *before* the birth of Christ there. When Jesus came, all of these "hopes and fears of all the years" were met *in Him* that night. What stirring memories lingered in the atmosphere of the little town the night Christ was born! It is still profitable today to explore its eventful history, because in its past are seen all the strains of human hope and need, of Divine love and compassion, which symbolize the great themes that surround the birth of Christ. There are four main events in the history of Bethlehem before the birth of Christ, and each of them symbolized a great truth that found its highest expression in the birth of Christ.

I. A PLACE OF SUFFERING AND SORROW

First, Bethlehem had already been a place of poignant *suffering and sorrow* before Jesus was born there. It was at Bethlehem that Jacob's beloved wife, Rachel, died while giving birth to their son Benjamin. In Genesis 35:19-20, we read, "And Rachel died, and was buried in the way to Ephrath, which is Bethlehem. And Jacob set a pillar upon her grave: that is the pillar of Rachel's grave unto this day." Rachel, you will remember, was the wife for whom Jacob served "seven years … (and then seven years more) and they seemed to him but a few days because of the love he had for her." What a loss her death was to him! The anguish of his heart over the loss still rung out in his dying words to Joseph, which were spoken years later: "When I came from Padden, Rachel to my sorrow died in the land of Canaan on the way ... and I buried her there on the way to Bethlehem" (Genesis 48:7).

Rachel had died in childbirth, while giving birth to a son. The boy was named from the cry that escaped his lips as she died. When she saw that it was a male child, she cried out, "Son of my sorrow!" Jacob altered it to "Benjamin," and the name became his for life. This strangely moving story is an eloquent prefiguring of another who would find in childbirth, and at Bethlehem, that "a sword (would) pierce her own heart also."

But surely there is even more in this story. According to the prophet Jeremiah, all the sorrows of Israel are wrapped up in the cry of Rachel and the sorrow and bereavement that surrounded her death. When the prophet Jeremiah saw the dreaded Babylonian Exile approaching, he saw the long line of Jewish captives being led northward from Jerusalem past Rachel's grave and he imagines hearing as they pass her grave the Mother of Israel still weeping for her children. In Jeremiah 31:15, we read, "A voice is heard in Ramah, lamentation and bitter weeping; Rachel is weeping for her children; she refuses to be comforted for her children, because they are not." We must remember, too, that these are the very words which Matthew quotes as he pictures the mourning of the mothers of Bethlehem after Herod's slaughter of the innocent children "two years of age and under, in and around Bethlehem." What does it all mean?

It is as though in Bethlehem all the sadness of mankind's predicament had found expression. There are human mortality and personal bereavement, delayed hope and bitter disappointment, moral conflict and deserved chastisement, national failure and inhuman cruelty, all gathered up in years of travail and tears that herald the coming of Him who would bring good tidings to the afflicted and bind up the brokenhearted. All the things that accompany human sin had been focused in Bethlehem's past before man's Savior *from* sin came through Bethlehem's manger onto the stage of history.

II. A PLACE OF SHARING

Second, Bethlehem was a place of the deepest kind of human *sharing*. It was at Bethlehem that one of the great human interest stories of all time, the story of Ruth and Boaz, was enacted. Thirty miles east of Bethlehem, in the direction of the Dead Sea, there lies the land of Moab and its lofty mountains. The Moabites bore a distant kinship to Israel, but they were always regarded by Israelites as being "heathen." In one of the friendly periods that developed between Moab and Israel in the days of the Judges, there went to Moab from Bethlehem, driven by a severe famine, a man named Elimelech. With him went his wife Naomi and two sons, one of whom later married Ruth, a Moabitess. After her husband's death Ruth returned with Naomi to Bethlehem, to adopt a new people and a new faith. She said to Naomi, "Entreat me not to leave you or to return from following you; for where you go I will go, and where you lodge I will lodge; your people shall be my people, and your God my God." Her vow and prayer were more than fulfilled. Ruth found a new home and a new happiness at Bethlehem, for she married Boaz and became ancestress of King David, and so of the Messiah.

The book of Ruth gives to the human race the loveliest religious romance in the world, and it all happened at Bethlehem. What a provocative thought, that before Jesus was born there, tiny Bethlehem already nourished in its history this great village love-story of Ruth the Moabitess, a heathen, and Boaz, the Israelite. The second strain that met in

Bethlehem the night Jesus was born was a strain of love, and even the kind of love that can receive and join itself to an alien, a stranger, a foreigner. We find here a prefiguring of Romans 5:8, which says that "God commendeth His love toward us, in that, while we were yet sinners, Christ died for us." Furthermore, the first two strains -- the suffering and sorrow of man which remind him of his sin, and the love of God, nearly came into violent collision at Bethlehem. King Herod, when he learned that a new king had been born in Bethlehem, decreed that all male children in Bethlehem two years old and under should be slaughtered, challenged the love of God. But God in His providence was not ready for the crucial encounter, so the baby Jesus was taken quietly out of Bethlehem to Egypt, awaiting the hour at Calvary when "in that dread act, the love of God and the sin of man would be tried."

III. A PLACE OF SOVEREIGNTY

Third, Bethlehem was historically associated with royal *sovereignty*. The third great event in Bethlehem's past centered around one of the great characters of the Bible, whose name is David. Neither Rachel nor Ruth could cast such glory on Bethlehem as did the luster of Israel's great King David. His story is one of the great stories of the world, and Bethlehem shares in it to the full. The little village of Bethlehem was the home of his youth. It was there that he remained tending the sheep of his father when the elders of the district welcomed Samuel the prophet-priest in his search for God's choice of a king. It was at Bethlehem that David, the young shepherd boy, was selected by Samuel to be Israel's next king.

In all the years that followed, Bethlehem remained famous as the early home of Israel's great king. In fact, in the announcement that the angels sang to the shepherds, it was declared that Jesus had been born in "the city of David." In the years after the death of David, the people of Israel had come to look to Bethlehem to produce another king, a son of David, to sit upon the throne of Israel. Over seven hundred years before Christ was born in Bethlehem, the prophet Micah gave this clear prophecy in his book: "Thou, Bethlehem Ephratah, though thou be little among the thousands of Judah, yet out of thee shall he come forth unto me that is to be ruler in Israel; whose goings forth have been from of old, from everlasting" (Micah 5:2).

In the sovereign providence of God, a decree from another throne, from the imperial throne of the Roman Caesar Augustus, brought Joseph and Mary to the appointed place at the appointed time, and the royal city became the birthplace of "the blessed and only Potentate, the King of Kings, and Lord of lords" (I Timothy 6:15). So the third strain that met at Bethlehem when Christ was born was the strain of royalty. As the poet said:

"There's a song in the air, There's a star in the sky;
There's a mother's deep prayer, And a Baby's low cry.
The star rains its fire while Heaven's angels sing.
For the manger at Bethlehem cradles a King."

IV. A PLACE OF SELF-SACRIFICE

Finally, Bethlehem was historically a place where a great act of *self-sacrifice* had been made. This was the last strain that comes from the history of Bethlehem that met at the birth of Christ. Without it, the Christmas story is incomplete. Without it, the portrait of Christ is incomplete.

This thread that was to be woven into the tapestry of Christ's birth also came out of the life of David. In II Samuel 23, there is recorded the story of a battle between David's army and a garrison of Philistines that had captured the town of Bethlehem. Beside the gate of Bethlehem was an old well, and the water had a flavor which David remembered from his boyhood. II Samuel 23:15 says, "And David longed, and said, Oh that one would give me drink of the water of the well of Bethlehem, which is by the gate!" And the next verse says that "three mighty men" of his army broke through the Philistine lines and returned to David with a simple, eloquent token of their readiness to die for him — a goblet of water from the well of home.

David was deeply moved, so deeply moved that he felt he could not drink the water. In II Samuel 23:17, we read his words, "Far be it from me, O Lord, that I should do this. Shall I drink the blood of the men who went at risk of their lives?" And he poured the water out on the ground as a libation offering to commemorate their heroism, bravery, and self-sacrifice for his sake.

This was the fourth and final strain that met at Bethlehem the night Christ was born — a kind of love that prompts the lover to utmost self-sacrifice, even to death. The cup that seemed to David red with the blood of heroic men, bound to him in a covenant of loyalty, obedience, and love, was to be filled again with the Blood of Another Sacrifice, sealing a still stronger covenant between the dying Savior and the men He loved until death. No man interprets the manger in Bethlehem correctly unless he sees hovering over it the dark and awful shadow of the Cross, the death-instrument on which the new-born Savior would one day volunteer His life unto death to save us from our sins.

There is a famous Dutch altar piece in a church in Amsterdam. It shows a crucifix hanging on the wall behind the manger at Bethlehem. It may sound like a strange combination to have the image of His death mingled with the joy of His birth, but how true it is! *Other men were born to live, but Jesus was born to die!*

At Bethlehem, all the strains of its own prophetic history came together when Jesus was born — the sad predicament of man's suffering and sorrow due to sin was represented there; the Divine love that accepts alien sinners and shares the total Divine estate with them was there; the royal sovereignty of Heaven was there; and the self-sacrifice that brings life was there — and all were revealed in Jesus. Wonderful Savior! Would you not have Him as your own? Receive Him into your heart by faith today. Join us, and "let us now go even unto Bethlehem."

THE MONSTER, THE MAGI, AND THE MONARCH

Matthew 2:1-12

    I. THE RAGING MONSTER

   II. THE REASONING MAGI

  III. THE REAL MONARCH

Chapter 3

THE MONSTER, THE MAGI, AND THE MONARCH

Matthew 2:1-12:

"Now when Jesus was born in Bethlehem of Judea in the days of Herod the king, behold, there came wise men from the east to Jerusalem, Saying, Where is he that is born King of the Jews? For we have seen his star in the east, and are come to worship him. When Herod the king had heard these things, he was troubled, and all Jerusalem with him. And when he had gathered all the chief priests and scribes of the people together, he demanded of them where Christ should be born. And they said unto him, In Bethlehem of Judea: for thus it is written by the prophet, And thou Bethlehem, in the land of Judah, art not the least among the princes of Judah: for out of thee shall come a Governor, that shall rule my people Israel. Then Herod, when he had privily called the wise men, enquired of them diligently what time the star appeared. And he sent them to Bethlehem, and said, Go and search diligently for the young child; and when ye have found him, bring me word again, that I may come and worship him also. When they had heard the king, they departed; and, lo, the star, which

they saw in the east, went before them, till it came and stood over where the young child was. When they saw the star, they rejoiced with exceeding great joy. And when they were come into the house, they saw the young child with Mary his mother, and fell down, and worshiped him: and when they had opened their treasures, they presented unto him gifts; gold, and frankincense, and myrrh. And being warned of God in a dream that they should not return to Herod, they departed into their own country another way."

Verse one says, "Now when (NASV, "after") Jesus was born in Bethlehem of Judea in the days of Herod the king, behold, there came wise men from the east to Jerusalem, Saying, Where is he that is born King of the Jews? For we have seen his star in the east, and are come to worship him." All three of the main characters of the chapter are introduced in this first verse — Jesus, Herod the king, and the wise men. Both Herod and Jesus are identified as "the king," and this title given to two persons creates the tension in the chapter. In this study, we will try to profile the three main characters.

I. THE RAGING MONSTER

One of the main characters in the story is a *raging monster* named Herod. Jesus was born "in the days of Herod the king." This sounds at first like an innocent historical reference to give a time-frame to the birth of Jesus, but it proves to be an integral part of "the Battle of the Ages." Herod is one of the most interesting and one of the most tragic figures of history.

Though Herod was known as "the king of the Jews," he himself was not a Jew. In fact, he was a hybrid, a half-breed non-Jew. His father was an Idumean, or an Edomite, a descendant of Esau. In the Bible, the Edomites are typically representatives of the flesh. Herod's mother was an Arab. The Arabs are descendants of Ishmael, about whom it was said,

"He will be a wild man: his hand will be against every man, and every man's hand against him" (Genesis 16:12). So the primary traits reflected in Herod's background are flesh and wildness, and those traits certainly reveal themselves in King Herod in the story of Jesus' birth.

Herod was an extremely paranoid man with a history of insane jealousy and suspicion. Anyone who reads his history should be prepared for a shock, because that history reads like a combination of the stories of Charles Manson and Ted Bundy. In fact, today Herod would be called a "serial killer." His biography is cluttered with strange murders. History holds Herod accountable for the murders of his favorite and most outstanding wife, Mariamne, their two sons, Alexander and Aristobulus, and a son by another marriage, Antipater. Earlier, he had killed Mariamne's brother and grandfather. All of these murders were in conjunction with alleged Jewish plots against Herod's throne. Augustus, the Roman Caesar, said that it was "better to be Herod's pig than to be Herod's son." When Herod knew that death was coming, he had about a dozen of the leading citizens of Jerusalem arrested, and he decreed that they be put to death when he died in order that there might be mourning in Jerusalem at the time of his death. It is a radical understatement to say that this King Herod was a spiteful, vengeful, violent man.

Jewish historian Flavius Josephus, in his <u>Wars of the Jews</u>, uses three words in describing King Herod. Conveniently for us, the words all begin with the letter "C." Josephus said that Herod was "capable, crafty, and cruel." These words are not difficult to substantiate in the personal history of King Herod.

First, he was extremely *capable*. He had great *military* capability. The Zondervan Bible Dictionary declares that "Herod showed himself the able master of varied types of war," and he was occasionally called upon to put down a Jewish revolt, which he always did with consummate skill. He had great *diplomatic* capability. One account declares that uncommon diplomatic skill was required for Herod to manage the complex situations he regularly faced – and survive. Then, he had great *oratorical* ability. He consolidated the Jews to himself with a combination of charm and oratory. Finally, he had great *building* ability. Anyone who has been to Israel has seen surviving evidences of Herod's bent toward construction. Herod built the great theater in Jerusalem. An extravagant palace stands just outside the southwest corner of the old city of Jerusalem as a monument both of Herod's building ability and his overweening egoism. Also, he rebuilt the Temple in Jerusalem, the very Temple which Jesus frequented during His public ministry. Herod also restored the old city of Samaria, and built the port city of Caesarea, which became the Roman capitol of Palestine. Further credits could easily be documented, but these are sufficient to prove that King Herod was an extremely capable man.

Then, Herod was an extremely *crafty* man. He has been described as "a cunning negotiator, a subtle diplomat, and an opportunist." As an example of his cleverness, we might cite his marriage to Mariamne. Herod had ten wives and over a dozen children, but Mariamne was his favorite wife. There is little question that Herod's marriage to her was a clever political move on his part. Mariamne was from a prominent Jewish family, the Hasmonean household. It surely gave Herod some credibility among the people he ruled when he married a "prize" from among the Jews.

Finally, Herod was an extremely *cruel* man. We have already seen some of the many evidences of his maniacal violence. His personal history was one of steady dispositional decline without restraint, and he became more and more prone to uncontrollable outbursts of violence. These outbursts were aggravated by delusions of persecution and political conspiracy. Herod died at seventy years of age, and the account of the birth of Jesus took place when he was sixty-nine. So he was pre-conditioned to react with swift and violent reprisal against the supposed threat to his throne that this "king of the Jews" would surely present.

The evidence of Herod's *capability* may be clearly seen in our text. "When Herod the king had heard" about the birth of a new king of the Jews, "he was troubled (agitated), and all Jerusalem with him. And when he had gathered all the chief priests and scribes of the people together, he demanded of them where Christ should be born." He acted with typical speed and skill. He convened a quick session of the entire ("all") Jewish Sanhedrin to get the desired information about the "Messiah's" birth. The "chief priests" came from the Saducean branch of the Sanhedrin, and the "scribes" were from among the Pharisees. Herod convened them all to expedite his own plan of action.

Then, the evidence of Herod's *craftiness* and cleverness is also conspicuous in our text. He called the wise men to him "privily" to avoid the Jewish suspicions of him, and he convinced these men from the east that he had a desire to worship the new-born king, also (verse 8). Also, he craftily secured the information he needed while focusing the attention of the wise men on the *star* instead of the new-born king. After he had found out from the Sanhedrin *where* Jesus would be born (verse 6), he then tried to find out his age. "He enquired of the wise men diligently *what time the star appeared.*" He asked them how long ago they had first seen the star, surmising that this would tell him the approximate age of the child. Herod's expedient cleverness is evident throughout the story.

Finally, Herod's extreme *cruelty* is clearly demonstrated in the text. In verse 13, the angel told Joseph to take his family and flee to Egypt, "for Herod will seek the young child to destroy him." And verse 16 highlights his cruelty in graphic terms: "Then Herod, when he saw that he was mocked by the wise men, was extremely angry, and sent forth, and slew all the children that were in Bethlehem, and in all the coasts thereof, from two years old and under, according to the time which he had diligently enquired of the wise men." As an aside, it might be noted that when men *abandon Christ*, it seems that they tend to *abuse children*. The long history of Herod's declining disposition and growing violence seemed to funnel in this one cameo act. It seems to be just that Herod would be renowned in history for this "Slaughter of the Innocents." King Herod could be called the "Adolf Hitler" of the Gospels.

This man of paranoid selfishness, morbid distrust, sick imagination, and "hair trigger" violence provides a stark and strange contrast to the other king in the story. One thing must be carefully noted before we move to the other key characters of the story. King Herod certainly received adequate evidence about Jesus. He knew that He was *"born King" (verse 2)*, that he would be a *"Governor" (verse 6)*, and that He was the *"Christ," or Messiah (verse 4)*. But he rejected the overwhelming evidence he had in favor of driving self-interest (the Biblical definition of sin). Herod *received* the *facts* about Jesus into his *head* (verse 6), but *rejected* the *faith* of Jesus from his *heart*. He was typical of the many people who accumulate great volumes of information about Jesus, but never come to know Him in personal relationship. Herod *studied the road map* – noting every detail of the highway – but *he never made the journey*. The raging monster would have found *ready mercy* if he had approached Jesus the way the wise men did, but instead he appears in the story as another tragic testimony of the deadly work of sin in human life.

II. THE REASONING MAGI

The second main character or group of characters in the story were the wise men, the *reasoning "magi,"* who came to honor Jesus at His birth. They are figures of some mystery, emerging like the star which they followed and then disappearing as quickly as it did. Several questions must be asked about these men if we are to fully realize the part they played in the story.

The first question is, Where were they from? If we can satisfactorily answer this question, we may have a handle on their identity and significance. The text tells us three times that they came "from the east" (verses 1, 2, & 9). Charles Spurgeon said of these men, "It is not possible to tell perfectly where they came from. Their native country may have been so distant that the journey occupied up to two years after the star appeared — verse sixteen. They may have come from Persia, or India, or even from China." Mr. Spurgeon was right in the first two statements, but he was probably far too extravagant in pushing the country of these men as far away as China. Personally, I have little question that they were from Chaldea, or Babylon, and I will explain my reasons for believing this.

The second question is, Who were these men? The title given them is "magi," from which we derive our modern words, "magic," "magicians," and "magistrates." But these men were not magicians in a dark and evil sense. They were quite respectable men of their time and place. Research shows us that they were scholars and scientists, skilled in several academic disciplines. They were students of (at least) history, philosophy, and astronomy, and normally such men were skilled in several other fields of study as well. Whoever they were, we must say without question that they had received *a considerable volume of very important information*. It is beyond imagination that they could have (or would have) done what they did without great information and great substantiation.

To shorten a long trail, let me quote from the book of Daniel (2:48): "Then the king (Nebuchadnezzar) made Daniel a great man, and gave him many great gifts, and made him ruler over the whole province of Babylon, and chief of the governors over all the wise men of Babylon." Daniel was indeed a great man – a great man of God, and a great political and social leader of Babylon. In fact, Daniel actually served as Prime Minister of Babylon under *four different kings*, and was a controlling factor in the government during all four reigns. The "wise men" cited in the above verse were probably the counterparts of the wise men in the Christmas story, though some six hundred years separated them in time. The Book of Daniel became a very important book in Babylonian history as well as in our Bibles. Because of the importance of Daniel, the book of Daniel probably became part of the official archives of the Persian empire, and probably is the largest single factor in the coming of the wise men from the east to honor Jesus at His Birth. These men probably had been studying the book of Daniel, and especially the crucial prophecy of Daniel 9:24-27, which actually gives the exact time-frame of the Messiah's coming. Daniel's testimony thus was carried through the centuries so that now, six hundred year later, these scholars of history, philosophy, and astronomy had discovered the predictions of a coming Messiah/ruler who would be born in Israel.

The third question is, What had they learned which caused them to hazard such a long and difficult journey? They had learned about the true God. They had learned about an expected Messiah/ruler who was to be born in Israel. They had learned the time of His coming. And since there was a large Jewish community remaining in Babylon because of the earlier Babylonian captivity of the Jews, they may have had access to Balaam's old prophecy recorded in Numbers 24:17, which associates a "star" and a "scepter," and declares that both would be related to Israel.

So these were men of *reason*. They were certainly scholars of the highest learning. And they were men of *rank*. We know this because of the easy audience they were given with King Herod. Herod would not take commoners into such an audience. Then they were men of *riches*. They brought extravagant gifts fit to be given *by* kings and fit to be given *to* a king. Gold, frankincense, and myrrh were "coffer" gifts that would have been a credit to royal and affluent people. And finally, they were men of *risk*. They overcome great difficulties, great dangers, and great distance in making this journey to Bethlehem. One of the marks of true faith is its risk-taking quality. These men were men of true faith. They were not merely "wise men" in the eastern sense of scholarship; they were wise men in the fully-developed Biblical sense of the word "wise."

III. THE REAL MONARCH

The final main character in the story -- *the main character* -- is the person who is the *real monarch* of the story. "Where is he that is born King of the Jews?" They expected to find a person. This person was to be natural-born. And he was to be born a king. Years ago, a British author named Dorothy Sayers wrote a lengthy play on the life of Christ entitled, <u>The Man Born to Be King</u>. If Jesus was born to be king, and He is the King that the Bible declares Him to be, then every member of the human race was born to *follow* the king. The wise men revealed that they knew this king was to be followed and worshiped. When verse eleven tells us that they "presented unto him gifts," the text uses a word which occurs seven times in the New Testament, and each time, it is used in connection with *offerings made to God*. I say again, these men were party to some incredible and demanding information!

Four titles are given in our text to the Person who was the object of the wise men's search. In verse one, He is called "Jesus," the human name of the Son of God. The name "Jesus" publicizes His humanity and His mortality. It is this humanity that qualifies Him to die in order to *redeem* sinners unto God.

In verse two, He is called "King," His royal name. During the reign of Queen Victoria, two little English girls were talking about their Queen one day. One said, "I wonder what she is doing right now?" The other replied, "Oh, she's just reigning." Jesus is reigning in glory at this very moment.

Then in verse six, He is called "Governor". Kings *reign*, and Governors *rule*. At this very moment, Jesus is making wise dispatch of all matters entailed in the government of the universe. He is managing the affairs of even the renegade planet Earth, working things to the eventual highest good of His own.

Finally, in verse four He is called "Christ," or "Messiah." It is the work of a Messiah to *restore* twisted circumstances to their proper relationships. So it is the business of Jesus to redeem, to reign, to rule, and to restore.

When the wise men asked, "Where is he?" the Sanhedrin answered with a 500-year-old word of prophecy from the Old Testament. They said, "In Bethlehem of Judea: for thus it is written by the prophet, And thou Bethlehem, in the land of Judah, art not the least among the princes of Judah: for out of thee shall come a Governor, that shall rule my people Israel." R. C. H. Lenski, the great Greek and New Testament scholar, commented on this verse with as astute observation that pinpoints the responsibility of every man with regard to the real monarch in this story. Though Lenski directed his remark to the Jews, his charge fits every man. He said, "Every Jew down to this day is confronted with Micah 5:2 and the Sanhedrin's answer to Herod. The Jewish Messiah is an *individual*, and *not* the Jewish nation, as Judaism has so often claimed. His birth must occur in Bethlehem *and nowhere else*. These facts were clearly acknowledged by the entire Jewish Sanhedrin of that day. *If Jesus is not this Messiah, then let the Jew tell us what Micah 5:2 means and let him contradict both this prophet and his own Sanhedrin as well."* Dear friend, do yourself an eternal favor and investigate this story carefully! The story is as important as heaven, hell, and eternity!

The story could be called "A Tale of Two Kings." At its very heart is an incredible paradox. Foreigners from a great distance away came to worship "the King of the Jews," but those who were his own kinsmen and just a few miles away would not take the time or effort to travel *five miles* to see and acknowledge the Son of God! The wise men worshiped the one "born King of the Jews," but the *false* "king of the Jews" *tried to murder Him!* The *Herods* of life always approach Jesus with *wickedness* in their hearts, whether they express it passively or aggressively. But thank God, the *wise men* of life approach Jesus with *worship* in their hearts — and they always gain notice in God's Book!

Two boys were struggling at a table with a jig-saw puzzle which was giving them a considerable amount of trouble. Finally one of them suggested that they should look at the picture on the cover of the box. When they did so, they saw that it was a picture of some kind of royal procession, with a king, surrounded by his courtiers and soldiers. After studying it for a few minutes, one boy said to the other, "Oh,

I see what we've been doing wrong. We've got to put the king in the middle of the picture." So they abandoned what they had done so far, and they began again, this time putting the king in the middle. Almost at once the whole thing began to make sense, and instead of a puzzle, they had a picture. Does anyone doubt that this world has become a chaotic and apparently insoluble puzzle? But God intended it to be a picture! Working without reference to the master-plan with which he has been provided, man is in complete confusion, and has created a society which has seemingly no pattern or purpose. The solution, so obvious to Christian minds and so startling in its simplicity, is to put the rightful King, Jesus, at the center of heart and life. When this is done, God turns the baffling puzzle into a beautiful picture.

Every person holds one of two crowns over the head of Jesus — either the crown of crucifixion (the crown of thorns) or the crown of coronation. If you have been indifferent toward Him, or wrapped up selfishly in yourself, you have pressed the crown of crucifixion down upon His head. However, you can lift that crown from His Head by an act of repentance, and place the crown of coronation upon His Head by an act of faith. Would you repent of your sin and selfishness right now and tell Jesus that you are doing so. Then, turn in total trust to Him, receive Him into your heart by faith, and trust Him to forgive you, save you, and use you. In that act, you will join the ranks of the reasoning wise men.

Chapter 4

HEAVEN'S MONOGRAM
OR
GOD'S STANDARD PROCEDURE

Luke 2:8-12:

"And there were in the same country shepherds abiding in the field, keeping watch over their flock by night. And, lo, the angel of the Lord came upon them, and the glory of the Lord shone round about them: and they were sore afraid. And the angel said unto them, Fear not: for, behold, I bring you good tidings of great joy, which shall be to all people. For unto you is born this day in the city of David a Savior, which is Christ the Lord. And this shall be a sign unto you; Ye shall find the babe wrapped in swaddling clothes, lying in a manger."

The text opens with an account of a *sudden appearance* in a most unexpected place. "And there were in the same country shepherds bivouacking in the field, guarding guards (literal translation) over their flock by night. And, lo (a picture of their surprise), an angel of the Lord suddenly and unexpectedly stood alongside them, and the glory of the Lord (the Shekinah, the supernatural radiance that marks the manifest Presence of God) shone round about them; and they feared exceedingly great fear." The Holy Spirit doubles up words here, using different forms of the same word back to back. "They feared a great fear." In transliteration, they experienced a "megaphobia". The sudden sight shocked them to the core of their personalities.

Then there quickly follows the account of a *startling announcement* made to those lowly shepherds. "And the angel said unto them, Fear not: for, behold, I evangelize (Gospelize) to you a great joy, which shall be to all people." The announcement is a "Gospel": it is Good News. It is News that *stays* News — and it is *always* Good. Christianity didn't come into the world on the editorial page — it isn't merely another topic for our philosophical or cynical evaluations. It is *good news from God in the face of bad news about men.*

A little boy was in the Christmas pageant of his church. His only part was to say, "Behold, I bring you good tidings of great joy, which shall be to all people." He didn't understand his sentence because of one word in it. So after the rehearsal, he asked his mother what "tidings" meant. She answered, "It means 'news'." The night of the pageant, the church was full of people, and the little boy experienced stage fright. When his time was due, he forgot his line, but his mother's explanation came to him and he said excitedly, "Boy, have I got news for you — and everybody should hear it!" That's very close to what the angel said.

"For unto you is born this day in the city of David, a Savior — Christ — Lord." There is no punctuation between these words; the abrupt suddenness emphasizes each title. As "Savior", He answers to man's biggest problem, that of *sin's corruption.* As "Christ" (Messiah), He answers to the problem of *society's chaos.* And as "Lord", He answers to the problem of *Sovereign control.* The basic question of each person's life is, "Who is going to be boss — God or me?" Sin means you are "out of control" by trying to manage your own life. Mark this principle: To be self-managed is always to be self-damaged. This pattern of life, followed to its conclusion, will cause each sinner to "self-destruct." Salvation, on the other hand, means that you are "under (proper) control" by letting Jesus be Lord of your heart and life.

So the angel's startling announcement told of a wonderful *birth* ("born this day in the city of David"), a wonderful *Baby* ("Christ the Lord"), and a wonderful *benefit* ("Savior"). No wonder the shepherds got all excited!

Now, the immediate text. The angel said the shepherds would recognize the Baby by this strange affirmation: "And this shall be a sign unto you; Ye shall find the babe wrapped in swaddling clothes, lying in a manger." Let's dismantle — and reassemble — the text "line upon line".

"THIS SHALL BE A SIGN UNTO YOU"

We normally take these words to mean that this is to be the means by which the shepherds would detect the right child, but the meaning is much, much bigger than that! There are several Greek words which may translate into our English word "sign". In the previous chapter (Luke 1:62), when the parents and relatives of John the Baptist were trying to choose a name for him at his birth, the neighbors and cousins of Elizabeth "made signs to his father, how he would have him called." In this case, the word means "gestures," a means of communication that had to be used at that time because Zacharias, John's father, had lost his voice.

But the word that is used by the angels is the biggest, most monumental, most meaningful word possible. It is the word "semeion". Any thorough student of the New Testament will quickly recognize that this is the exclusive word used to define and describe the seven great representative miracles of Jesus in the Gospel of John. They are not mere miraculous acts performed by Jesus; they are "signs". Each of them addressed one of mankind's great problems, and signifies (signifies) God's answer to the problem. Also, the great "scandal-miracles" associated with Jesus — the virgin birth (Isaiah 7:14) and the resurrection of Jesus as pictured in the "whale-of-an-experience" of Jonah the prophet – are both labeled as "signs" (Matthew 12:39-40).

Why is this particular word used by the angel? What does it mean? Is there anything more here than the angel's identification of the accouterments by which the "born-Christ" would be recognized? Surely there is!

Let's look at a sample use of this word "semeion" elsewhere in the New Testament. In II Thessalonians 3:17, the Apostle Paul draws his letter to a conclusion with these words: "The salutation of Paul with mine own hand, which is the token in every epistle: so I write." The word translated "token" is our word "semeion". W. E. Vine in his Expository Dictionary of New Testament Words, says that Paul's greeting in his own handwriting is "his autograph attesting the authenticity of his letters." Note the word "autograph". This is what a "semeion" is. It is an autograph.

The same meaning beautifully applies in our text. The "sign" specified by the angel in Luke 2:12 is Heaven's autograph; it is God's monogram, His signature, His brand-mark, His label, His mark of genuineness, His seal. So here in a feed bin of a cattle stall in a cow shed in Bethlehem of Judea is Heaven – signed, sealed and delivered! Here is Heaven's

Monarch – but in a humble manger! Here is the King of all Kings – nestled in straw in a feeding trough for cattle! This is Heaven's imprimatur. Here is the Family Crest of Heaven lowered to the filthy crust of this planet earth. Frederick Godet, the Swiss Bible scholar, in his commentary on Luke's Gospel, says at this point that "this sign has nothing Divine about it except its contrast with human glory." I wonder if Mr. Godet truly realized what he was writing! The phrase, "except its contrast with human glory", takes us to the "significance" of Luke 2:12.

    What is the worst of all sins? Negatively it is unbelief, or the refusal to centralize your life around its proper, intended center, Jesus Christ. You may not like this arrangement, but the truth is that you don't get a vote. Someone Else set the rules of the game of life long before you arrived, and the only reason any human being cannot recognize their validity is that he is too ignorant or too impudent to admit what is best for him. Positively, the sin of unbelief may be recognized as pride. This sin, with its negative and positive sides, is the mother sin, the father sin, the parent sin, of all other sins. This sin constituted the Fall of Satan in heaven. This sin comprised the Fall of Adam and Eve in the Garden of Eden. This sin constructed hell! This sin consigns human beings to banishment from God forever. C. S. Lewis called pride "The anti-God state of mind", and he was right!

    Dear friend, don't hurry past this idea. If you are without Christ, either passively or aggressively, you are possessed with an anti-God state of mind. Jesus presented this truth in a passage of incredible contrasts when He said, "For God so loved the world, that he gave his only begotten Son, that whosoever believeth in him should not perish, but have everlasting life. For God sent not his Son into the world to condemn the world; but that the world through him might be saved. He that believeth on him is not condemned: but he that believeth not is condemned already, because he hath not believed in the name of the only begotten Son of God" (John 3:1618). The aggressive unbeliever deeply resents this arrangement because he wants to set his own rules. This is what all religion is about. It is man setting his own rules — this time, about *God*! It is man in his God-hunger telling God that he has figured out the way to approach God, and if God doesn't agree, He should! But the bad news is that man doesn't get a vote in the matter. He is not nearly as smart as God (read the book of Job about this point sometime). The Good News, however, is that God has answered every problem of disqualification that man has, and has clearly set forth His Solution (Romans 3:25; Galatians 3:1). When any human being becomes aware of that solution, his choices are clear-cut: he will remain in unbelief as a rebel against God, guilty of high treason against the Throne of the Universe, or he will humbly receive Christ and the Gift of Eternal Life through Him. These are grave issues, and they deserve a gravity of heart which suits their seriousness.

If pride is the worst sin of all sins, then what is the highest virtue man can know and practice? If the worst sin is pride, then the highest virtue must be humility. Humility is the "pro-God state of mind". When Aurelius Augustine was asked, "What is the first Christian virtue?" he replied, "Humility". Then he added, "And the second Christian virtue is humility, and the third as well."

Is there any pride in Heaven? None whatever. Heaven has never been contaminated by the sin of pride. Then what is the very atmosphere of heaven? What is the "attitude" of heaven? It is *humility*. So God would never have regarded Bethlehem's cow trough as a reduction, as a condescension, as a stooping-down, as a humiliation. I think God is right at home in a barn! Is that too daring for our minds which are so dizzied by pride? But isn't this the way heaven always acts? Yes! Yes, it is! God's heart is always humble. No wonder His continuous activities are giving and serving! No wonder His vocabulary is full of "grace", "love", "mercy", "loving-kindness", etc. No wonder He is so scorching in His antagonism toward anything that smacks of pride. You see, the Lord Almighty is not out to *hurt* your pride — He is out to *kill* it!

The Birth of the Baby in Bethlehem is "Heaven's Monogram", God's "sign" of all of this. No wonder, then, Madeline L'Engle could say, "Can I bear this extraordinary birth without breaking apart?" The answer to her question is *no*! Either I will break apart in humble faith before God, or I will break apart in self-condemnation and self-destruction. I may not like those alternatives, but again, *I don't get a vote*! Sin has complicated life by just this much, and it is deadly serious, and eternity big. The world doesn't "break apart" before God — and then experience His glorious reconstruction, the New Birth — because it is either totally ignorant of the Event of Bethlehem (increasingly the case in twentieth-century America), or it has rejected the explanation of it, choosing rather to either wrap Christmas in a halo of sickening sentiment or rebelling against the Divine Content of it altogether. In either case, humanity at large is failing to read God's sign. May God help us to rightly read the sign, because this sign points us in the right direction and will take us to our true home for Christmas!

"YE SHALL FIND THE BABY"

This is the first sentence of interpretation after the word, "sign". Now we *know* we are on the right track in the way we read the sign. The Lord God Almighty, in the Person of His Eternal and Preexistent Son, at one tiny point of time has passed from Pure Spirit to a sub-visible beginning of a human being — in the warm womb of a virgin mother! God has reduced Himself to the size and shape of an ovum in a human mother's womb! After conception He multiplies materially many times over to become a human zygote, then a fetus, then a born infant, then a child, then an adolescent, then an adult, the God-Man. Incidentally, shouldn't we be awfully careful in handling this miracle that recurs daily on a lesser scale, the miracle of the birth of merely human babies?! Remember "the Baby"!

> "They were looking for a King,
> To slay their foes and lift them high,
> But Thou camest, a little baby thing,
> That made its mother cry."

Russian history tells us that Peter the Great, one of Russia's most renowned Czars, at one time during his reign, shed his royal garments and traveled incognito to Amsterdam, where he dressed himself in peasant garb and worked for some time as an apprentice shipbuilder. There was never a minute during this time that he was not the Czar of Russia, but his true identity was not recognized. And so it was with Jesus. It is as if God had landed behind enemy-occupied lines. And He landed "in disguise"!

Remember, humility is heaven's lifestyle. This is God's eternal method. This is God's style, God's standard, God's scheme. Here is the *modus operandi* of the Eternal God in an innocent sounding line of Scripture: "ye shall find a baby". You see, there is no definite article in that sentence. It is not "the baby", as the King James Version says; it is "a baby", which further illustrates that this is heaven's monogram. Here is heaven's Great Champion — but He is *burping* instead of *blustering*! That's a bit "too much" for us, isn't it?

Jesus modeled the sign, the "Baby" style, throughout His Life. Once when His disciples were arguing to protect themselves from the performance of a menial service, someone gestured in amazement toward Jesus, and lo, He had taken off His regular clothes and had wrapped (remember that word!) Himself in a towel, had poured water into a basin, and was getting down on the floor to wash their feet! What is that but a mockup of His eternal history? He sat in glory at God's right hand throughout eternity past, rose up, put off His usual garments, girded Himself in our humanity, poured out His blood, and began to wash our sins away. Afterward, He went back up, dressed Himself in His original garments, sat down again, and resumed His position in the humility of heaven.

Do you want a seal for the sign? Then, give careful attention to this truth. When John the Baptist introduced Jesus at the Jordan River, he called him "the Lamb of God". Peter, in turn, said that "we are redeemed ...with the precious blood of Christ, as of a Lamb without blemish and without spot." In each case, the word "Lamb" is the usual generic word for that animal. But John uses the word twenty-eight times in the last book of the Bible (the book that unwraps some of heaven's true glory), and he doesn't use that normal generic word at all. Get ready for this world in a word: He uses the diminutive form of the word, which means "a little pet lamb". Great God our Father, could it be that all of heaven bows to "a little pet Lamb"? The bowing of myriads of people from every kindred, tribe, people, and nation — to "a little pet Lamb"? The chorusing cantatas of eternal song celebrating "a little pet Lamb"? A diminutive form at the center of all that magnitude and majesty! We scarce can take in this breathless truth. Heaven is built on *littleness* instead of *largeness*, on *humility* and not *haughtiness*, on *serving* instead of *strutting*! No wonder Jesus said, "He who would be great among you, let him be the servant of all."

Joyce Kilmer, in his poem entitled, "Kings", wrote:

> The kings of the earth are men of might,
> And cities are burned for their delight,
> And the skies rain death in the silent night,
> And the hills belch fire all day.
>
> But the King of Heaven, Who made them all,
> Is fair and gentle, *and very small*;
> He lies in the straw, by the oxen's stall
> Let them think of Him today."

Oh, that men might think of Him today! Think truly, think accurately, think intelligently! When Thomas Arnold was the famous headmaster at Rugby School, a boy brought a paper to him which contained a badly messed-up math problem. After Arnold examined it, he said tenderly to the boy, "Son, you must think!" The boy replied, "But, sir, I did think." Arnold remonstrated, "Then, son, you must think again, only this time you must think correctly."

Friends, that is the precise meaning of the Biblical word, "repentance". It means to rethink the basic reality of things, only this time you think from God's point of view. Jesus is called the "logos", or "logic" of the universe (John 1:13). "In Him are hid all the treasures of wisdom and knowledge" (Colossians 2:3). To be away from Him is to be unwise and ignorant, no matter what your IQ. One day soon, a great *unveiling* (the exact meaning of "Revelation", the name of the last book of the Bible) is coming. Then, the cobwebs of life will be swept away, and we will see into the very heart of things. Meantime, we submit ourselves to the simple sovereign, the Lamb of God.

A little boy was walking with his father down the street of a large eastern U.S. city. They came to a block where a skyscraper was being constructed. They stopped for a minute to observe the workers and their work. As they raised their eyes toward the top of the building, they noted all the naked girders piercing into the sky, and the workmen, reduced in size by their distance from the ground, moving skillfully over the girders. Suddenly, the little boy pointed upward and asked, "Daddy, what are those things moving around up there?" The father smiled and said, "Son, those are men." A moment later, the boy said, "Daddy, the closer men get to heaven, the littler they get, don't they?" Exactly! We reduce and reduce, following the "Baby cue", until it's as if we went through a point of oblivion – to emerge into the glory of the far side. Indeed, when it is over, we will wish we had "found the Baby"!

"WRAPPED IN SWADDLING CLOTHES"

Weigh these words carefully. "Wrapped" – here is God "all wrapped up". He is enclosed, confined, contained, limited. Madeline L'Engle wrote, "What presents me with problems with Christmas is not the secular world with its cotton-bearded Santa Clauses, its loudspeakers belching out Christmas carols the day after Thanksgiving, not the shops full of people pushing and shouting at each other as they struggle to buy overpriced Christmas presents. No, it's not the secular world which presents me with problems about Christmas — it's God. He willingly limited His unlimitedness, put the wrapping of mortality over His immortality, accepted all the pain and grief of humanity, submitted to betrayal by that humanity, was killed by it, and died a total failure (in human terms) on a common cross between two thieves. What kind of flawed, failing love is this?"

You see, there it is again! God crosses our proud path and begins to heave all of our categories, all of our values, upside down. He throws everything into topsy-turvy disarray. This is precisely why the world *stops* at the Manger. It won't let Jesus grow up! He is too great a threat to our daily procedures. He places the "manger danger" right in front of our own self-centered sovereignty. It is fitting that babies should be in cribs – tiny, clinging, helpless. But this Baby was born to be a king. This is what Herod could not stand when the wise men said to him, "Where is He that is born King of the Jews?" He saw Jesus as a rival to his own throne, and he moved to abolish Jesus by killing all male children two years of age and under in and around Bethlehem.

Dear sinner, you have the same problem. Living in your own private kingdom, you cannot easily allow a rival king to vie for your throne. But you have a bigger problem. Self as king is Satan's lifestyle, and his final abode will be the Lake of Fire (Revelation 20:10). Selfishness alone, though innocent in appearance, places you in total opposition to God's standard, makes you Satan's companion, and will unite you to him forever. This is the reason Nathaniel Hawthorne called egotism or selfishness "the bosom serpent" in every person's heart. Think of the contrast — God on a Cross, tiny as a man, clinging to nails, gasping for breath, pathetically weak (II Cor. 13:4, "crucified through weakness") — *and doing this as a heavenly strategy*! This is sometimes more than we can adjust to.

Notice that this Baby was "wrapped in swaddling clothes". One version of the Bible actually paraphrases the verse to read, "swathed like a mummy". Swaddling clothes are burial clothes. They are strips of cloth, normally linen, normally about a foot wide, and the word means "tightly wrapped", like a mummy. All the way through His life, heaven spells it out that the highest standard of life is in someone giving himself up for somebody else, strictly confining himself to *somebody else's welfare,* whether by living of by dying. That is the ultimate in humility.

Years ago, there was an Abyssinian statesman named Blater Heroni. He was the Abyssinian representative to Paris when the Treaty of Versailles was formed to end World War I. He was a Christian, and had just translated the entire New Testament into the language of his people. When he arrived in Paris, he quickly realized how impossible it seemed for the world to have peace. He began to wonder how it could happen. His recent studies in the New Testament brought into sharp focus the impossibility of having peace without the Prince of Peace. The ideas formed creatively in his mind, and he conceived a picture. He approached a Parisian painter and explained his idea. The outcome is a masterpiece.

The painting shows the world broken into two pieces like an eggshell broken into two halves with jagged and erratic edges at the point of the break. However, it is the smooth parts that face each other and the broken edges that face away from each other. So the break looks hopeless and irreversible. The painting thus shows a fragmented world with two giant hemispheres turned defiantly away from one another. There is a large gap between the two parts, and they are suspended in separation. But here is the genius of the painting. Between those two hemispheres, there is a Cross with the Son of God hanging on it. He is dying in agony, but there is a strange aura of glory about His face. Instead of the blood dripping downward toward the foot of the Cross, the blood runs outward from His hands and flows upon every continent of the torn, divided world, painting them red with the color of redemption.

Heaven's Monogram shows Jesus wrapped in the clothes or garments of death, the epitome of a suffering God Who reigns from a Tree. Occasionally people refuse positions of service for Christ by saying, "I just don't want to be tied down right now." Can we really serve a Christ who was nailed up for us if we refuse to be tied down for Him? Jesus was born with the shadow of death over His cradle, and it darkened into the horrors of Calvary at the end. And this is heaven's lifestyle. Heaven is constructed not merely around the Lamb, but around the Lamb in a certain character, "the Lamb as it had been slain".

"LYING IN A MANGER"

Into a stinking stall in a stable, God came. And it wasn't because He couldn't arrange a palace, or the best maternity suite, but because He *chose* tiny Bethlehem and the feed-trough of the cattle in a barn as His point of approach to mankind. How peculiar!

One of my favorite writers is the late C. S. Lewis. Of all his works and the writings of other authors about Lewis, my favorites are still his children's stories called The Chronicles of Narnia. The last book in the series of seven is called The Last Battle, which won the Carnegie Medal for the best children's book of 1956 and is the best written and most sublime of all the Narnia stories. Any reading order is possible for the other six, but The Last Battle must be read last from any standpoint if the reader is to "see" the point of the others. When the books are read successively in a short time, the last one has a terrible beauty, an "eternal" reality, that makes the heart ache, break, and shout at the same time. The climax of the book begins at a stable door (!) – that's right, at a stable door. At one moment, the stable door seems to represent death, at another moment it seems to represent salvation, at another it suggests the doorway to all reality, at another the entrance to eternity – but remember, it is a *stable* door. C.S. Lewis had apparently studied Heaven's Monogram carefully. Heaven's Family Crest is a stable door! God's Signature is a stable door! The archetypal ensign of Glory is a stable door! And not a professional, oak-paneled door; just a roughhewn stable doorway, such as Jesus Himself might have made as a teenage carpenter in Nazareth! All reality entered the world through a stable door and was deposited in the feed-bin where cattle eat! And according to Lewis, the final dispatch of all issues is made at a stable door where God Almighty sets up shop and holds His Last Judgment. No wonder he chose to call it "the last battle". All — *all* — ultimate battles are fought at a stable door. "He is sifting out the hearts of men before His Judgment Seat" – at a stable door.

I was standing in a hospital corridor with an anxious family one day, when the doctor emerged from the Intensive Care unit and said hopefully, "Finally, we have been able to stabilize his heart. His heart is stable again." *"Stabilize . . . . stable"?* May I dare to change the context of those words, while only slightly varying their meaning? The big question for Christmas (indeed, for *every* day) is, "Do you have a *stable heart?"* Have you been through the *stable door?* Have you applied to the Lord of Life by faith so that He could *"stabilize"* your heart forever? Has God changed your heart so you can fit into *His* scheme of things?

All human hearts resolve into two categories. One says, "Not Thy will, but mine, be done." The person with that heart joins Satan's selfish brigade — and marches defiantly into hell. The other says, "Not my will, but Thine, be done." That person joins Jesus and goes to heaven, to join his humble but happy hallelujahs to those of a throng that will forever celebrate the wonder of "the little pet Lamb".

TOO GOOD TO BE FALSE

Luke 2:10-11; "And the angel said unto them, Fear not: for, behold, I bring you good tidings of great joy, which shall be to all people. For unto you is born this day in the city of David a Savior, which is Christ the Lord."

I. WHERE

II. WHEN

III. TO WHOM

IV. WHO

V. HOW

VI. WHY

Chapter 5

TOO GOOD
TO BE FALSE

Luke 2:10-11:

"And the angel said unto them, Fear not: for, behold, I bring you good tidings of great joy, which shall be to all people. For unto you is born this day in the city of David a Savior, which is Christ the Lord."

One of my favorite Christmas stories is a quaint short story by Bret Harte, a story which doesn't seem to be about Christmas at all. It is entitled "The Luck of Roaring Camp." A poor prostitute, the only woman in Roaring Mine Camp, died in childbirth. The only legacy she left behind was the new-born baby, and since the men weren't sure who its father was, they all felt responsible to take care of the baby. The baby's "cradle" was a candle-box on a pine table; but the men quickly realized that such a box was not fit for a baby's crib, so they sent one of their members eighty miles on a mule to Sacramento to get a rosewood cradle. When the cradle came, the men then realized that the rags on which the baby was sleeping seemed out of place. So, the man was sent back to Sacramento to purchase some clothes—lacy, frilly clothes. When the baby was dressed in its lovely new garments and placed in the rosewood cradle, the men observed for the first time that the floor was dirty. So, they scrubbed it clean. Then they noticed that the walls and ceiling were also dirty. So, they scrubbed them and whitewashed them. Later, they mended the windows and put drapes on them. And, because the baby needed to be quiet at times, they remained still and ceased their rough language and rowdy ways. In fact, they slowly dropped their bad language and bad conduct because of the baby's presence in the camp.

When the weather permitted, they took the cradle out to the mines, and then they discovered that the mining area also had to be cleaned and flowers planted to make the surroundings as lovely and as attractive as the baby. Finally, the men themselves began to improve both their inner character and their outer appearance. Thus, the coming of a baby resulted in the regeneration and transformation of Roaring Mine Camp into a new and attractive place filled with new and attractive people. When these previously rough miners began to realize the change produced among them by the baby, they declared that the baby had brought "the luck" to Roaring Camp, so they named him "The Luck." The story becomes even more similar to the Gospel story when the baby dies tragically at the end, thus fixing the redemption of the camp through the baby's death as well as through his life.

Surely this story explains itself as a Christmas story!

Writing in his Just-So-Stories, renowned author Rudyard Kipling said,

> "I keep six honest serving men
> (They taught me all I knew);
> Their names are What and Why and When
> And How and Where and Who."

Someone referred to these six questions as the "six editorial friends," and another called them "the journalist's five W's and one H formula." Again, the questions are, "What, Where, When, Who, How, and Why." A writer who ignores these six questions cannot possibly give an adequate account of any story he is trying to tell.

Almost all of these "editorial questions" are vividly answered in Luke's dramatic telling of the Christmas story. We will re-examine the story through the frames of these questions.

I. WHERE

First, the account tells us *where* the first Christmas story took place. "In the city of David," the angel announced (vs. 11). Verse four says that Mary and Joseph "went up from Galilee, out of the city of Nazareth, into Judea, unto the City of David, which is called Bethlehem." The term, "the city of David," denotes royalty and suggests that the baby born there that night would be a king.

A Penn State University football player (a defensive tackle, probably) was asked, "Where was Jesus born?" "In Lancaster?" he asked tentatively. "*Lancaster!* Of course not!" the questioner exclaimed. "Pittsburgh?" he asked meekly. "You gotta be kidding," the questioner said disgustedly, "Any idiot should know that Jesus was born in Bethlehem." The player said with a shrug, "Well, I knew it was *somewhere in Pennsylvania!*" Most Americans are at least aware that Jesus was born in Bethlehem, though their awareness of the message and the meaning of Christmas often goes no farther than that.

It was certainly no accident that the birth of Jesus occurred at Bethlehem. God even governed the mind and action of a Roman Caesar to arrange for Mary to be in Bethlehem at the time of the baby's birth! And God had governed previous history for many centuries to place just the right ingredients in the atmosphere of Bethlehem.

It was at Bethlehem that Jacob's wife, Rachel, had died while giving birth to one of Jacob's sons, Benjamin. So, *death and birth* were already associated together centuries before Jesus was born at Bethlehem. Indeed, it was birth that came out of death!

It was at Bethlehem that Boaz, the "kinsman-redeemer," had purchased the lovely Ruth and lavished his love upon her. So, *redemption and romance* were already associated together at Bethlehem centuries before Jesus was born.

It was at Bethlehem that David had stood with his army and looked out across the battle lines of the barbarian Philistines and had nostalgically rehearsed his boyhood days. Suddenly he said, "Oh, for a drink of water again from the well of Bethlehem, as I had so often in my boyhood days." Three of David's "mighty men" heard his plaintive sigh and, without consulting their king, they surprised the Philistines in a lightning raid and brought back to David a container of water from the well of Bethlehem. David was so overwhelmed with surprise, pleasure and gratitude over their deed of devotion that, in honor of them and their act, he refused to drink the water but solemnly poured it out on the ground as a libation offering. So, *sacrifice that produced satisfaction* had already been witnessed at Bethlehem long before Jesus was born there.

> Life out of death!
> Romance out of redemption!
> Satisfaction out of sacrifice!

Can anyone fail to see the preparation of history which God had made at Bethlehem to further explain the meaning of the birth of Jesus?

Furthermore, the name Bethlehem means "House of Bread." Here the great "grain of wheat" (John 12:24) was born which would later be crushed between the upper millstone of God's judgment against sin and the lower millstone of hell's fury against holiness – and Jesus would be "baked" through the furnace of Calvary into the Bread of God which gives life to the world.

Note carefully *where* it took place and give careful attention to *what* occurred there.

II. WHEN

Then, Luke tells us *when* the story took place. The angel said "this day" in verse 11. Verse one tells us that "this day" was during the reign of Augustus as emperor of Rome, and verse two tells us that it was during the tenure of Cyrenius as governor of Syria. So, "this day" was about 2,000 years ago. How exciting the announcement of "this day" should have been to the shepherds, but the fact that it was 2,000 years ago should be very *embarrassing* to *us*. Though the Good News announced by the angel was to be relayed to "all people," 2,000 years later we are forced to sadly admit that 2.3 billion people have still never heard the Name of Jesus, and many more of those who have heard His Name still have never had a satisfactory witness about Him.

Queen Victoria once asked an English military leader, "If I were to announce something that should be universally known throughout the world, how long do you estimate it would take us to get the message to every nation and reasonably to every person on earth?" After a time of careful thought, the man replied, "Your Majesty, I think we could accomplish the task in 18 months." Then what shall we say about ourselves, about the church, about the world Christian community when we continue to engage in extremely self-centered, self-indulgent consumer Christianity (especially in America) instead of turning all of our resources outward to total world impact? We are often like guests at a Tupperware party, appraising the goods and making our self-pleasing selections instead of living a "martyr-witness" lifestyle (Acts 1:8) to make Christ known "unto the uttermost parts of the earth."

One wonders how long God will allow our self-entertaining exercises to continue before He "brings down the curtain" on the American Christians' "consumer party." Embarrassingly, the WHEN of it was 2,000 years ago.

III. TO WHOM

Then, the story announces *to whom* the Good News was directed. In verse ten, the angel said, "which shall be to all people." And verse eleven concentrates the universal address of verse ten by saying, "unto you." The message was directed "to all people," generally and universally. But, "all" includes *each*, so it is particularly directed "to you"—and you—and you—and you. It is to be repeated "to all people" until each "you" has been informed. And when it comes to *you*, it is God's plan that it be repeated through you on its way "to all people." When God becomes real in your life, it is His intent to come through you on His way to "all people." Are you available for God to convey His good tidings to all people—through you? Do you have serious dreams and plans for taking the glad tidings to some of the "all people" who have never heard?

IV. WHO

The message of the angel also tells us *who* came on the first Christmas. "Who is Christ the Lord," he announced. What an ecstatic and electrifying announcement it was!

The word "Christ" is the Greek word for the "Messiah." What a peculiarity! An angel of Heaven broke through the veil and announced that the 18-inch-long baby laid in straw in a cowshed in Bethlehem was none other than the long-promised, long-prophesied, long-predicted, long-expected, long-awaited Messiah of Israel. He was the One appointed and anointed in Heaven, and anticipated and announced on earth. Micah 5:2 had foretold that He would be born in Bethlehem, Isaiah 7:14 that He would be born of a virgin, Isaiah 53 that He would die a violent death for sinners (the description of the Cross is so vivid that the writer might have been writing while looking at it, though the account was written over 700 years before Jesus was born), and Isaiah 9:6 tells us that His Name would be called Wonderful Counselor, Mighty God, Everlasting Father, and Prince of Peace; and that in time the government of the world would be upon His shoulders. All this was packed into the frame of a tiny baby in Bethlehem!

And, He is also identified as "Lord." This is the translation of the word "Jehovah," which means that the tiny baby is God. THAT TINY BABY WAS GOD! And He is Lord—Lord of everything and everybody! With regard to human beings, this means that every man and woman who has ever drawn a breath will be appraised, evaluated, measured and judged solely in terms of his or her personal relationship with a Carpenter from Nazareth Who was born as a Baby in Bethlehem! You see, Jesus is as much Lord of a non-Christian as He is of a Christian! Your agreement or disagreement with it does not change the Fact of His Lordship; it only determines whether you have joy or judgment, pardon or perdition, Heaven or Hell.

The question is *not* "*Will* you acknowledge Him as Lord?" but "*When* will you acknowledge Him as Lord?" for one day, as surely as God lives (and you have no vote about that either!), "every knee will bow before Jesus, and every tongue will confess that Jesus Christ is Lord, to the glory of God the Father." (Phil. 2:10, 11). Whether the knee and the tongue belong to a rebel, a cynic, a skeptic, an agnostic, an atheist, or an infidel, *every* knee will be bent in acknowledgment of Jesus as Lord and *every* tongue will acknowledge His Lordship.

What does this Lordship mean practically in the life of a person who gladly accepts it?

(1) It means that Jesus has the *right* to *control* you;

(2) It means that Jesus has the *responsibility* to *correct* you; and

(3) It means that Jesus has the *resources* to *compensate* you.

Have you gladly accepted "Christ the Lord"? In 1952, Princess Elizabeth (as she then was) went to Kenya Colony (as it then was). A few days after she left England, her father, George VI, died. Immediately she hurried home from Africa. The moment she stepped off the plane at London Airport, she stepped onto British soil as queen in her own right. But, for fifteen months she remained uncrowned. Then, on June 2, 1953, she was crowned Queen of England. In the person of their representatives, every member of the British Commonwealth bowed before her and kissed her scepter, acknowledging her as their rightful queen. She had her coronation day. Has Jesus had that in your heart? Oh, He is King in His own right; but have you "crowned Him Lord of all" in your life?

A Christian father was playing the piano one Sunday afternoon and singing Gospel songs with his children in their home. They sang, "Serve Him, serve Him, all ye little children; God is love, God is love," then, "Love Him, love Him...," then, "Praise Him, praise Him, all ye little children; God is love, God is love." There he stopped, but his little girl said, "Daddy, you forgot to ' crown Him!'" Jesus is King of the Universe, but your heart may still vainly hold out as a "rebel province" against Him. Would you bow before Him at this very moment and acknowledge Him as King of your heart? *Who* came on the first Christmas? "Christ the Lord!"

V. HOW

Then, the angel's announcement tells us *how* He came. He was "born," the angel said. "Born!"

Put the word "God" and the word "born" together and see what a mystery, what a marvel this is. I Timothy 3:16 says, "Without controversy great is the mystery of godliness; God was manifest in the flesh." This is, without question, the greatest of all miracles. The greatest miracle is the Person of the Incarnate Christ. That the nature of God and the nature of man were united without fusion or confusion, that Jesus was both God and man in one Person without any loss on the part of either nature, that He was fully (100%) God and fully (100%) man (and still only 100%, *not two persons*) – this is the greatest miracle of all. So, the supreme and superlative and supernal miracle is the moral, personal miracle of the Personhood of Jesus the God-man.

Think of it again! The Son of God leaves the bosom of His Heavenly Father and nurses on the breast of an earthly mother. The Son of God becomes (also) the son of Mary. Thus, the Most High God becomes the most nigh God. The Infinite becomes an infant! The Infinite becomes intimate – with us! The Infinite becomes definite – in a baby! The God who had always been only pure spirit now adds visible and tangible substance – the substance of actual human flesh –to His Nature!

Jesus was the Heavenly Child of an earthly mother, and the earthly child of a Heavenly Father! In eternity, He had a Father, but no mother; in time, He had a mother, but no father! He made His own mother! He was older than His own mother, and exactly as old as His Father (to our minds, the word "age" and "old" suggest beginning, deterioration, and change. No, Father and Son were *eternal*!) He was co-eternal, co-essential, co-existent and co-equal with His Father – but now He is also human! "Veiled in flesh the Godhead see, Hail His incarnate Deity." No wonder the "herald angels" sang!

What is the meaning that we can detect in this mystery? It means that God Himself has become human for our sakes. Human! As truly *human* as He is *eternally Divine*. Very God of very God, but also man. So, Jesus is the perfect revelation of what *God* is like, and the perfect revelation of what *man should be like*. He is the perfect manifestation of both God and man, and the model and measure of every man. John Phillips wrote, "The great mystery of the manger is that *God* should be able to translate Deity into humanity *without* either *discarding the Deity* or *distorting the humanity*."

Again, what does this practically mean for us?

(1) It means that Jesus is fully identified with me – *even* with my sins, though He Himself was not guilty of sin.

(2) It means that Jesus, being both God and man, is the only qualified Mediator, or Middle-Man, between God and man.

(3) It means that from His conception and birth as a human being, for the very first time in all of God's Eternal History, He now has a mortal nature, a nature capable of dying. The universe is the stage, Jesus is the Script; our redemption is the plot, and with His Birth, the stage is SET!

All other babies were born to live, but Jesus was born to die. *How* did He come? He was "born"!

VI. WHY

Finally, the angel's announcement happily tells us *why* He came. Let the spotlight of Heaven fall on the word, "Savior."

"Unto you is born this day a Savior." Man's Great Problem and God's Great Provision meet in the word "Savior."

The word "Savior" indicates a problem. Because man is *in sin*, he is *"out of sync"* with God. There is a popular Christmas quote that is appearing more and more in Christmas messages and on Christmas cards. It is a marvelous statement, but it has one grave problem about it. Here is the quote:

> "If our greatest need had been information,
> God would have sent us an educator.
> If our greatest need had been technology,
> God would have sent us a scientist.
> If our greatest need had been money,
> God would have sent us an economist.
> If our greatest need had been pleasure,
> God would have sent us an entertainer.
> But our greatest need was forgiveness,
> So God sent us a Savior."

A great quote – until the punch line. The truth is that man's greatest need is *not* the need for forgiveness. Forgiveness is a neutral concept. Forgiveness only "clears the decks" for the real action. Forgiveness creates a *blank*, but God wants to re-create each of us into a *blessing*—according to His clearly-defined intention. Jesus did not say, "This is life eternal, that men may be forgiven." No! As strategic and crucial as forgiveness *is*, it is *not* our greatest need. "This is life eternal, that men may know the only True God, and Jesus Christ whom Thou hast sent" (John 17:3).

Man's greatest need is a full, free, warm, wonderful relationship with God. A relationship that is defined as union (and communion) between God and man. A relationship in which the character of God so infects the redeemed nature of man that redeemed man thinks like Jesus, talks like Jesus, loves like Jesus, rejoices like Jesus, and willingly dies like Jesus – all in behalf of other lost human beings! This relationship is not possible without the forgiveness that removes the impediment *to* the relationship, but forgiveness stops far short in defining man's greatest need. As a "Savior," Jesus doesn't merely offer us a clean slate (a blank), but a script for the most dynamic adventure ever known among men.

Suppose that a king makes a decree of a full pardon to all prostitutes. This is good news, but it guarantees no change of lifestyle. But suppose the same king then asks one of the prostitutes to become his bride (see Romans 7:4). The lifestyle of a queen is far superior to that of a prostitute (even a *reformed* one)!

Jesus was a teacher, but He was far, far more than that. Jesus was a physician, but He was far, far more than that. Jesus was a prophet, but He was far, far more than that. Jesus was a priest and a king, but He was far, far more than that. Dear friend, Jesus Christ is *less than nothing* to you if He is not *first of all your Savior*. And He is not your Savior if He is not *more than all* to you. The word "Savior" has both negative and positive sides to its meaning. Negatively, it means that Jesus can *take out* of your human heart everything that *sin* has put *into it* (and finally will do so for every redeemed saint); and positively, it means that Jesus can put back *into* the human heart everything that sin has taken *out* of it—and MUCH, MUCH, MUCH MORE! So, the word "Savior" is a word identifying God's Full Provision for man's foul problem. It includes salvation *from* sin, and salvation *to* sainthood, service and similarity to Jesus.

Let me illustrate both the negative and positive sides of our salvation. First, the *negative* side, the *removal of sin*. In the popular "Peanuts" comic strip, Lucy went once to Linus with a piece of paper and a pen in her hand and said to him, "Linus, would you sign this paper? It absolves me from all guilt." In the next frame, Lucy has gone to Peppermint Patty and said, "Peppermint Patty, please sign this paper. It absolves me from all guilt." In the next frame, she has approached Schroeder (the cultured piano-player) with the same request. Then she goes to Charley Brown with the same request. He takes the pen and the paper, but says, "What does this mean? What is this for?" Lucy answers, "No matter what happens, any place or any time in the world, this absolves me from all blame." In the last frame of the cartoon, Charley Brown says philosophically, "That would be a wonderful document to have."

Good news! Every saved person, every born-again believer, every redeemed sinner has such a document! It was drawn up and signed in Heaven, sealed on earth by the blood of Christ, and miraculously applied to the need of the broken-hearted sinner by the Holy Spirit. Its record is in the Bible, and its reality is experienced in the New Birth. To some, it is incredible, too good to be true. But believe it or not, no matter what happens, at any place or at any time, I am absolved fully, finally, freely and forever from all guilt and blame – because Jesus Christ is my own personal Savior, and His Blood has made full and final payment for my sins. "Gone, gone, gone, gone; yes, my sins are gone!"

But there is an even *more* glorious *positive* side in the salvation Jesus provides. I not only receive a *pardon* that negates my sin (and neutralizes my life), I receive *purpose, peace, and power* as well! The purpose is *to be like Him* in character *and conduct* (to impact the whole wide world by the teaching and training of others according to His plan and pattern); the peace is both vertical and horizontal; and the power is His enablement for the fulfillment of all of His purposes. Now, the illustration.

Many high school students read the George Eliot novel entitled <u>Silas Marner</u> because of an assignment in an English Literature class. Like most legal assignments, it left the student without appreciation for the great document he had read.

Silas Marner was a man who had soured on life because of hurt and disappointment. Bitterly wounded by unjust treatment in a previous residence, he had moved to a new community where he sadly refused open relationship with anyone. Though consumed with dark bitterness, he engaged in a profitable weaver's vocation and acquired a small personal fortune of gold pieces which he stored in a "safe" in the floor of his small house. Every evening he would take out his gold, run it through his fingers, count it, and love it. As a compensation for his deep wounds, he made gold his private god and greed his personal motive. The account of how he was saved from his love of gold is a great illustration of a Christian's salvation from the love of sin.

One night, when Silas left his horde of gold unguarded for a short while, a drunken thief broke into his home and stole it. Silas Marner was not saved from his love for gold by having his gold stolen. It *was* stolen, but he actually loved his money just as tragically – and even more – when he was penniless as he did when he had all of his gold securely hidden away. Neither is a sinner saved from his sins merely by having his sins taken away in Christian conversion. In fact, he may find a taste for sin recurring *after* he is saved just as it was *before* he was saved.

So how was Silas cured of his love of gold? One extremely cold winter night, he came into his modest home from an errand. He had left a bright fire burning in the fireplace because of the cold of the night. As he entered the room, he saw something on the hearth before the fire that shimmered and glittered with golden color in the light of the fire. His heart began to beat wildly. He was so obsessed with the love of his lost gold that gold was all he could think about. He thought the thief had repented and returned his gold. He got down on his knees to run his fingers through it and cherish it once more. But his fingers did not touch the gold of money. He ran them instead through the golden curls of a little girl's hair. Her mother had perished in the bitter cold outside, but she had seen the light and come to Silas Marner's house, had crept inside, shut the door, and had fallen asleep in front of the fire. In succeeding days, Silas Marner adopted her, and little Eppie stole steadily into his heart with her disarming love. By and by, his love for gold began to die. He became so full of a living love for this little girl that there was no room for the old deadening love of gold anymore. His entire life was transformed. The evil of his deadly love for gold was overcome and replaced by the good of a larger and better love.

Sinners are saved from sin in the same way. Jesus is the Lamb of God who takes away our sins, but He does not leave us forever a blank. Having taken away our sins, He then gives us the Life of His Person, the Liberty of His Power, the Luxury of His Possessions, and the Legacy of His Purpose. Hallelujah, what a Savior!

No wonder the angel called it "good news." It is *good* because it came out of the nature of God, and it is *news* because it actually happened. This is news that remains news – and it is *always only good news!* No human being could invent this story because it is beyond our highest creative powers. And nobody would believe it unless it was true. However, when a person plumbs the depths of this "gospel," he discovers that it is actually *too good to be false*.

Dear friend, if the Holy Spirit has made you aware that you have a serious problem – you are away from God and helplessly lost in sin, the answer to your problem is in Jesus the Savior. As you frankly admit your sin, come to Jesus and trust Him today to work the miracle of His salvation in you —to remove your sin, and to replace your love for sin with greater love of the Savior.

"Though Christ a thousand times in Bethlehem be born,
If he is not born in you, your heart is still forlorn."

"Holy Child of Bethlehem, Descend on us, we pray,
Cast out our sin and enter in, Be born in us today."

THE FIRST CHRISTMAS GIFTS

(Matthew 2:11)

I. The PREPARATION of their gifts
   A. Their unique pattern
   B. The usual perversion

II. The PROTECTION of their gifts
   A. The threat of distance
   B. The threat of danger
   C. The threat of demands

III. The PRESENTATION of their gifts
   A. To Christ Himself
   B. At cost to themselves

IV. The PROVISION of their gifts
   A. They overcame the hostility of Herod
   B. They underwrote the flight to Egypt

V. The PREMONITION of their gifts
   A. They foretold His history
   B. Their gifts were fulfilled in Him

Chapter 6

THE FIRST CHRISTMAS GIFTS

Matthew 2:11:

"And when they were come into the house, they saw the young child with Mary his mother, and fell down, and worshipped him: and when they had opened their treasures, they presented unto him gifts; gold, and frankincense, and myrrh."

It is fascinating to note that the three greatest events in the life of Christ are all given a close association with material and financial things in the New Testament. At the Cross, the Roman soldiers gambled over the seamless robe of Jesus. Paul had hardly completed his great apologetic chapter on the resurrection when he said, "Now concerning the collection . . ." (I Corinthians 16:1). And here, the wise men who came to worship Christ after His birth brought lavish and valuable gifts.

Christianity has been called "the most materialistic of religions" because of its emphasis on the *importance* of material things and of *individual stewardship* of material things. It is estimated that Jesus talked six times more about money than about Heaven and Hell put together. So it is fitting that we should examine the gifts, as well as the meaning of the gifts, which the wise men brought to Jesus.

The gifts of the wise men were the first Christmas gifts ever given. Indeed, the wise men were the first Christian givers, and a studious examination of their gifts will reveal that their giving provides an excellent model for all Christian giving. They show to all Christians the way to give.

I. THE PREPARATION OF THEIR GIFTS

First, note the *preparation* of their gifts. These men were "wise" because of the way they prepared the gifts which they brought to Bethlehem. The preparation they made provides a pattern for all Christian givers. Verse 11 contains this phrase: "When they had opened their treasures." It was surely no accident that they had "treasures" for Him when they arrived in Bethlehem. Apparently, considerable forethought and advance action had gone into the gifts that were chosen and brought to Bethlehem.

The wise men knew that they were going to present gifts to a King (Matthew 2:2), therefore they did not leave it to chance. If chance or caprice had determined their gifts, or if they had chosen at the whim or fancy of a moment, they would not have had such gifts to give when they arrived in Bethlehem. How wise every Christian would be today if he practiced the same preparation in his Christian giving.

These wise men did not dishonor Jesus by giving him their economic leftovers. One Oriental Christian evaluated the stewardship of many American believers in these words, "Americans seem to treat God as their garbage can, or in the same way they would treat their dog or cat. They consume what they want, then give the leftovers to Him." I would call that "scrap stewardship." It is like throwing leftover scraps across a barnyard fence to the chickens.

The First Christmas Gifts

In the book of Malachi, the last of the Old Testament books and one of the greatest books in the Bible on the subject of stewardship, the prophet severely condemns this inferior kind of giving to God. The problem is that this kind of giving occurs only by default, if at all. If this Christian's budget includes God, He is placed at the bottom of the list. Every other bill is paid first. This Christian often excuses his poor giving by saying, "But I am in heavy debt, and it is only reasonable that I should pay my debts first." The truth is that you *are* in heavy debt—but you are in debt *to God* first of all! This person wrongly estimates that God will not prosecute any failure to pay, but their creditors will! God prosecutes poor stewardship by confining the one who practices it in the narrow closet of a sour self.

A wealthy old man had gathered his family for their annual family reunion. He looked around the banquet table into the faces of his sons and daughters and each of their spouses. Then he wistfully said, "Not a *single* grandchild! Not *one*! Not one of you has presented me with a grandchild. Why, I'd give a million dollars to the first one of you that gives me a grandchild to bounce on my knee." Then he bowed his head to say thanks for the meal. When he raised his head, only he and his wife remained at the table!

Money is very important to everybody, and your money is very important to God—but not for the reason you think! It is not for God's sake that you should practice good stewardship—it is *for your sake!* God sees your money as coined personality. Your money represents *you*. And He knows that the way you spend your money is the perfect index to your character. Indeed, I will go so far as to say that, if I can regularly read your check stubs or your credit card receipts, I can tell you where you will spend eternity!

In Matthew 6:33, our Lord told us to put God and His Kingdom first in our lives. This means first in every area of life, first in our total lives (including the way we secure, save, spend, and share our money). In I Kings 17, Elijah was sent to a widow who lived in the village of Zarephath. A famine had just begun to grip the land of Israel, and it proved to be a long famine. The widow was to care for Elijah during the rest of the drought. When he arrived at her home, Elijah found her out gathering sticks and he told her that he had come to stay with her. She told him that she was gathering sticks to build a fire, and that she was about to use the little amount of meal she had left to prepare the last meal before she and her son would die. The text then says, "And Elijah said unto her, Fear not; go and do as you have said: *but make me thereof a little cake first*, and afterward make cakes for yourself and your son. For thus says the Lord God of Israel, The barrel of meal shall not waste, neither shall the cruse of oil fail, until the day that the Lord sends rain upon the earth." The woman believed the prophet and served him first, and, as always, God kept His promise. That story is a permanent parable of stewardship. The faith that puts God first has always been honored by Him, and that kind of faith has broken up more than one famine!

We may be certain that the wise men did not come to Bethlehem and then say, "We're coming to a young King and we should bring gifts for him. What do we have handy that we might give?" No! They had prepared their gifts a long time before they arrived. Indeed, they prepared them before the journey began. And today, our regular gifts to Christ should be prepared, prepared *first*, and prepared *in proportion* to the way He has blessed us. No one is too poor to give a regular proportion, *beginning* at the minimal Biblical level, if that person will only put God first. These men were wise in the preparation of their gifts, and so should we be.

II. THE PROTECTION OF THEIR GIFTS

Second, these men were very wise in their *protection* of their gifts. In fact, they would never have arrived with their gifts if they had not protected them.

They protected their gifts over a long *distance*. I believe that they came from Babylon or Persia. This possibility best fits all the facts of their case. This means that they had to travel over one thousand miles to get to Bethlehem, and in those days, that would have been a very, very (*very*) long trip! This may account for their late arrival (Joseph, Mary, and Jesus were living in a *house* by this time, and Herod specified *two years of age* as the possible age of the child). Furthermore, much of this distance (possibly 300 miles) would have been through desert terrain, where bands of marauding thieves would find it easy to victimize travelers. Carelessness in their journey would easily lead to the loss of their gifts.

In the same manner, protection is required today to guard the gift that should be presented to the Lord. For many people, the greatest distance in their lives is the distance between the pay counter and the collection plate! One humorist said, "Money talks, all right, but in my experience, it has a very limited vocabulary—it only says, *'Goodby!'*" Our gifts to God must be given before all of our money says a last "farewell."

Closely akin to the problem of distance is the problem of *danger*. In fact, distance and danger may be synonymous perils. The distance increases the danger. In our stewardship as Christians, we must be aware that there are thieves lurking everywhere to steal the gifts that should be given to God. For example, the thief of *pleasure* approaches, seeking to rob us of the gift that belongs to God. Or the thief of *need* arrives to make such pathetic (but supposedly "sensible") claims upon us. Like the man who went down from Jerusalem to Jericho in Jesus' parable (Luke 10:25-34), we discover that we have "fallen among thieves" as we go to worship Jesus.

Furthermore, the sheer *demands* of the trip might have made a claim on the gifts they had brought to give to Jesus. If the trip was as long as I believe it was, it was very costly financially. The expenditures involved in travel, food and lodging and incidentals along the way, might have made claims on the valuable gifts they brought. The farther they went on the long trip, the more conscious they became of the demands of long travel.

Someone said, "An income is something difficult to live within, and impossible to live without." I heard of a businessman who succumbed to financial emergency while on the "long trip" of financial necessity. He had apparently proven himself over the "long haul" by operating a successful business for many years. But then, his financial affairs took a sudden turn for the worst. Due to unforeseen circumstances and changes in the local economy, his business rapidly began to fail. After some time, he had been brought almost to despair by the failure. He called a wise friend to ask him for advice. The friend said, "Take a beach chair and your Bible, and go down to the ocean side. Place the chair at the edge of the water and sit down in it. Then, open your Bible and place it on your lap. Let the wind blow the pages until they stop. Then, look down at the page, and the first thing you see will give you the advice you need." The desperate man quickly obeyed this counsel.

Several months later, the businessman took his wife and two daughters with him to visit his wise friend. The businessman was wearing a new Italian suit and an expensive pair of new shoes. His wife was wearing a full-length mink coat, and his daughters were wearing beautiful silk dresses.

"My goodness!" exclaimed his wise friend. "My advice seems to have worked well. Tell me what happened." The businessman answered, "Well, I took your advice. When I sat on the beach with my Bible open on my lap, I waited until the wind stopped blowing the pages. My Bible was open to the book of Hebrews, but the only thing *I saw* was *"Chapter Eleven"!* You see, it is very easy for self-centered people to use a plea of poverty or indebtedness to their own advantage when "good fortune" turns to bad!

But these wise men carefully protected their gifts. Today, money is often transferred from place to place in armored vehicles. An armed guard often stands by where money changes hands. We, too, should give attention to the protection of our gifts to God. The wise men were not embarrassed when they arrived in Bethlehem, and neither should we be when we look into Christ's face with the gifts we have brought to Him. They protected the gifts they brought to Jesus, and so should we.

III. THE PRESENTATION OF THEIR GIFTS

Thirdly, these men were wise in the *presentation* of their gifts. The text says, "And when they had come into the house, they saw the young child with Mary his mother, and fell down, and worshipped him: and when they had opened their treasures, they presented unto him gifts."

These men were wise enough to give their gifts *to Christ Himself.* Note that they came to where Jesus was. A Christian's gifts should be given where Christ is alive and Divinely advertised. Every Christian should seek out such a church, and there they should give their gifts. Note, too, that "they presented *unto him* their gifts." They did not give their gifts to a religious movement or a cause.

We can be sure that they did not lay these gifts at Mary's feet. We must be very firm here, because there is a widespread movement under foot to elevate Mary to a position of equality with Jesus. It is interesting to note that "the young child" is mentioned four times in Luke 2 without reference to anyone else with Him, and the phrase, "the young child and his mother" is used five times, and always in that order. If some people on the scene today had written that chapter, they would have given supremacy to Mary, even in the order of the words in the text. But these wise men presented unto Him their gifts. We may be sure they properly honored Mary, but they did not worship her or unduly exalt her. When we decide to give, we should not ask, *"To what cause should I give?"* but rather, *"To Whom?"*

We have already been reminded that they gave these gifts *at great cost* to themselves. Andrew Fuller was the British pastor who agreed to "hold the ropes" while William Carey went down "into the dark pit of heathenism." One day Fuller was soliciting funds for Carey and the work in India. He approached a Christian gentleman about the matter, and the brother said, "Well, Brother Fuller, seeing it is you, I'll give five English pounds." Fuller answered with great earnestness, "Seeing it is I, you will give nothing! But seeing it is the Lord Jesus Christ to Whom you are giving, how much will you give?" The man accepted the rebuke and the challenge and said, "Seeing it is the Lord Jesus Christ, I will give fifty English pounds." Would you give if *Christ* stood before you with extended hand to receive the gift? How *much* would you give if *He* received your gift from your hand?

Years ago, Dr. Elmer Stackhouse was making missionary appeals in Canada and pleading for offerings for the work, and a great amount of money was given to the missionary cause. At the close of one service, a little lame woman hobbled up to the preacher and handed him a beautiful diamond ring. She said, "I have no money, but this is a ring Mother gave me just before she died, saying that some day I might need it. But I want to give it now." Dr. Stackhouse answered sharply, "Why, my dear lady, I couldn't let you give me that ring!" and he pressed the ring back into her hand. The little lame lady serenely answered, "Dr. Stackhouse, I'm not giving the ring to *you*. I'm giving it to *Jesus!*" That was different. The preacher reached down and took the ring.

There is an old legend entitled "Why the Chimes Rang." It tells the story of a set of church chimes which rang only when someone offered at Christmas a gift that came from the heart. The rich gave their gold—no, they gave *some* of their gold—but the chimes were silent. The not-so-rich gave "what they thought they could afford"—and the chimes did not ring. Finally there came a lame boy who had no money at all; he laid his crutches on the altar—and the chimes rang loud and clear! When I finished reading the legend, I had the suspicion that it was left incomplete. I'm sure that the boy left the church with a new strength inside and out, and I'm even more sure that God was pleased. Sacrificial giving to God *always rings the bell!*

Friends, our giving is only Christian when we give our gifts to Christ Himself. We should never give to anything less—merely to a cause or to a church or to a collection. Our gifts should be given as if they were place in His pierced hand. And they should be given with the same spirit of devotion manifested in the wise men. They "worshiped Him" as they gave their gifts. Indeed, they worshiped Him *by giving their gifts*, and so should we. They were wise in the way they presented their gifts to Jesus.

IV. THE PROVISION OF THEIR GIFTS

Fourth, let's see the *provision* which was made for Joseph, Mary and the Christ-Child through their gifts. The wise men did not know that their gifts would be used for such an incredible purpose when they brought them to Jesus, but God knew, and that is really all that matters.

They knew nothing of the hostility and dishonesty of King Herod when they inquired of him in Jerusalem where the Christ-Child would be born. The "worship" he pretended he wanted to give would have turned to murder if he had seen the Child. But the Heavenly Father knew this, and so He went to Joseph in another dream and ordered him to take his family and make a hurried journey to Egypt. But Joseph and Mary were very poor. How could such a trip be financed?

The situation seemed impossible—except for the gifts of the wise men! "Where God guides, He provides! Where He reigns, He sustains!" The word "provide" (*pro video*) and its related form, "providence," means "to see in advance," but it also includes the *meeting* of the foreseen need. Joseph, Mary and Jesus were sponsored by God, out of Heaven's *providence*, but the "delivery agents" were these men from the east who were wise enough to obey God and follow the guidance He gave them. Their gifts could easily be negotiated into sufficient cash to finance the Divinely-directed trip to Egypt.

Today, there are many places Christ wants to go to, but He doesn't have the necessary "travel expenses" because He depends upon His Body, and not enough members of that Body are wise enough to bring their best gifts to Him. But remember, God does prosecute poor stewardship. Today, we are having to pay in taxes what we would not voluntarily give to God. Indeed, every war that is fought all over the world occurs because Christians refused to finance Christ's arrival in all the "Egypts" of the world. Millions of people on planet earth are starving, either physically or spiritually or *both*, because there have not been enough wise men and women to give their gold to Christ to bring the needed nourishment to them. You cannot open your newspaper or magazine or watch a newscast without seeing where Christ would go if He had the necessary funds to make the trip. Do not misunderstand this point. God is not a beggar, and He is only dependent upon His people by sovereign choice. "We are workers together with God" (I Corinthians 3:9)—by His choice. The partnership is absolutely "lop-sided"; He carries the heavy end, but He still chooses to use us. He may "own the cattle of a thousand hills" (and everything in the hills as well), but He puts the ownership and stewardship of the cattle and the hills in our hands, and He expects us to use the cattle for His glory and our good.

It was not more important or imperative that the Christ-Child be taken to the safety of Egypt "in the days of Herod the king," than that He be taken, through the Gospel and all of its related ministries, to the places of human need that are so conspicuous all over the world today. The gifts of the wise men made provision for the needs of the Son of God, and so our gifts will do today.

V. THE PREMONITION OF THEIR GIFTS

Finally, look at the *premonition* of their gifts. It is significant that the wise men offered more than just prayers and adoration when they "fell down and worshiped him." They arrived bearing gifts for the "King of the Jews." Gift-giving for royalty was an ancient custom. A notable example occurred when the Queen of Sheba brought gifts to King Solomon on her visit to Israel (II Chronicles 9:1-12). Psalm 72:10-11 reveals that the Messiah too was worthy of extensive (and expensive) gift-giving. These wise men surely brought their gifts to honor the ancient tradition of presenting worthy keepsakes to noted monarchs. But there is much, much more in this story than the mere serving of custom and tradition.

The gifts of these wise men were unconscious predictions, or prophecies, of the person and work of Jesus Christ. Thankfully the wise men did not bring the Child a toy, or a silver spoon, or a teething ring, or a pacifier. They didn't bring a cute little outfit for His circumcision. Nor did they bring clothing or flowers for His mother. They brought gifts which revealed more about the Christ-Child than they could have imagined. Though they were following the inclinations of their hearts, surely God presided over their choices.

"When they had opened their treasures, they presented unto him gifts; gold, and frankincense, and myrrh." One little Sunday School boy described the gifts as "gold, frankenstein and mermaids." Another called them "gold, circumstance and mirth." In all seriousness, we should examine each of these gifts with great care. Without violating the freedom of the wise men, the selection of their gifts was nonetheless engineered by God, and thus there is perfect coordination between their gifts and the entire Person and work of Christ. The first two gifts that are mentioned, "gold and frankincense," suggest something about *who Jesus is*, and the third gift, "myrrh," suggests *what He did*.

The first-named gift, "gold," symbolized *spiritual sovereignty*. Gold has always been a symbol of royalty, and is invariably found among the possessions of royal persons and families. Here, the gold symbolized both the royal lineage of Jesus stretching all the way back to King David, and His rightful Person and position as universal "King of Kings." The giving of the gift of gold at His birth suggests that He was *born to rule and to reign as King*. This certainly correlates perfectly

The First Christmas Gifts

with what the angel had said to Mary about the Child's birth: "The Lord God shall give Him the throne of His father David, and He shall rule over the house of Jacob, and of His Kingdom there shall be no end."

Think of the personal and practical meaning of this for you and for me. Jesus is King over everything, and He has a King's right in our lives. He has the right (and will assume the responsibility) to exercise full authority over your life and mine.

The second gift that is mentioned is "frankincense." Frankincense was an aromatic gum resin used for incense by the priests of Israel. "Pure frankincense" (Exodus 30:34) was a primary ingredient in the holy incense that was used in Israelite worship in the Old Testament tabernacle and in the Jewish Temple. The Old Testament priests burned frankincense during their prayers to God, and the incense that was used became a symbol of the priestly office and the prayers of those who filled the office. This incense was never to be used for private or ordinary use (Exodus 30:34-38).

The giving of the gift of frankincense to Jesus at His birth suggests that He was born to function as a priest before God; He was *born to represent man before God.* Thus, this gift suggests the *spiritual service* of the Son of God.

The Latin word for priest is *pontifex*, which means "a bridge-builder." The chief role of a priest is to build bridges between God and people. Unconsciously, the wise men acknowledged that Jesus would be a bridge-builder between God and man. And indeed, the New Testament presents Him as One Who built bridges instead of barriers.

Think again of the personal and practical implications of this truth for your life and mine. Those who follow Jesus Christ are also called to be priests or bridge-builders for all men. Every Christian is called upon to practice a "ministry of reconciliation" (II Corinthians 5:19-20) among men whose sins have separated them from God, and build bridges across the chasms that separate and divide men from each other.

The last of the wise men's gifts was "myrrh." Myrrh is a spice which was used to embalm the dead for burial. Imagine bringing this to a new-born baby! However, it was perfectly fitting that it should be brought to Him at His birth, because He was born to die! His life was bracketed by death. Myrrh was not only given to Him as a gift at His birth, myrrh was also mixed with wine and offered to Jesus as He was suspended in agony to die on the Cross (Mark 15:23), and myrrh was one of the spices used by Nicodemus to prepare the body of Jesus for burial (John 19:40). So this gift suggests the *spiritual suffering and sacrifice* of the Son of God. He was *born to redeem men to God* by His Death on the Cross.

Again, think of the personal and practical implications of this truth in our lives. Every Christian is to see himself as a "dead man walking," crucified with Christ and thus dead to self. Also, each Christian is called upon to live a life of passionate love and devotion to Jesus Christ.

Someone said, "The *real* Christmas tree is a Cross." At that Tree, God loved us enough to give His Very Best. The Gift that was given at that Tree is the only eternally important Gift that has ever been given. The real Christmas *gift* is Jesus Christ. And the residual effect of that Gift when received into a person's heart is eternal life. And when That Gift—"eternal life through Jesus Christ our Lord" (Romans 6:23) is "unwrapped" in personal experience, it breaks up into a multitude of blessings in the life of the one who receives it.

THE SALVATION STORY

Galatians 4:4-7: "But when the fullness of the time was come, God sent forth his Son, made of a woman, made under the law, To redeem them that were under the law, that we might receive the adoption of sons. And because ye are sons, God hath sent forth the Spirit of his Son into your hearts, crying, Abba, Father. Wherefore thou art no more a servant, but a son; and if a son, then an heir of God through Christ."

I. It is the Story of God's Ideal MOMENT, 4a.

II. It is the Story of God's Ideal MAN, 4b

III. It is the Story of God's Ideal METHOD, 4:4c

IV. It is the Story of God's Ideal MODEL, 4d

V. It is the Story of God's Ideal MOTIVE, 5

VI. It is the Story of God's Ideal MIRACLE, vs 6

Chapter 7

THE SALVATION STORY

Galatians 4:4-7:

"But when the fullness of the time was come, God sent forth his Son, made of a woman, made under the law, To redeem them that were under the law, that we might receive the adoption of sons. And because ye are sons, God hath sent forth the Spirit of his Son into your hearts, crying, Abba, Father. Wherefore thou art no more a servant, but a son; and if a son, then an heir of God through Christ."

Very soon, a major motion picture will be released, based on C. S. Lewis' fantasy story, <u>The Lion, the Witch, and the Wardrobe</u>, one of the seven "Chronicles of Narnia." These popular children's fantasy stories (with mature Christian content) present incredible illustrations of Christian truth, and should be read again and again by every Christian.

In the first of the "Chronicles" to be made into a movie, a traitor named Edmund (a picture of Adam selling the human race into a course of destruction to satisfy his own indulgence) has been redeemed by the death of a lion named Aslan (a type of Christ, the "lion of Judah"). I must hasten to add that, as in the salvation story, the lion comes back to life after his death. After the redeeming death and death-shattering resurrection, accomplished for the traitor, the two girls of the story, Susan and Lucy, are discussing the incredible events.

"'Does he know,' whispered Lucy to Susan, 'what Aslan did for him? Does he know what the arrangement with the Witch (who represents Satan) really was?' 'Hush! No, of course not,' said Susan. 'Oughtn't he to be told?' said Lucy. 'Oh, surely not,' said Susan. 'It would be too awful for him. Think how you'd feel if you were he.' 'All the same I think he ought to know,' said Lucy. But at that moment they were interrupted."

The discussion between Lucy and Susan illustrates the dilemma of the typical Christian today. The typical Christian is basically illiterate of "the great transaction" of Christian salvation in its many glorious dimensions (you see, *literacy of reading is not gained by listening to **someone else** read; the 'reader' must learn and articulate the subject himself*). The full message of salvation, on the one hand, is so horrible, and on the other hand, so happy, that no person should be given a "half dose" of this Medicine. If he receives only the horrible part, he will have an inaccurate view of God and the Gospel. He will only think of Christianity in terms of "always telling a struggling man of his sins and the judgment of God." If he receives only the happy part, he will never appreciate the marvelous Radical Rescue of Divine salvation, and he will tend to think of God as a Cosmic Bellhop who exists to meet his every whim and to make him happy.

In this study, I would like to give an overview of God's glorious salvation. It is not intended to be exhaustive, but merely suggestive. It is my hope that this study will initiate a quest in the reader's heart to fully explore all the dimensions of God's salvation. What is the nature of the salvation story?

The Salvation Story

I. It is the Story of God's Ideal MOMENT, 4a.

First, the salvation story is the story of an ideal *moment* selected and prepared by God. Verse four tells us that it was "when the fullness of the time had come" that God acted. The underlying conviction behind this phrase is that God is perfectly sovereign over time and history. The text calls it "*the* time," not merely *a* time, or *any* time. You could certainly say that adequate Divine premeditation and preparation had gone into the development of the time. The word "fullness" (*pleroma*) means exactly that; the time was pregnant with Divine preparation and was ripe for Divine action. The womb of time, impregnated with God's Big Purpose, had been swelling for centuries. Now the gestation time was over. The time of birth (The Birth) had come.

Brilliant South African author Alan Paton once wrote, "If we wait until the time is *ripe*, we probably won't start until the time is *rotten*." The time of Jesus' coming into the world was both rotten and ripe; indeed, its rottenness was a part of its ripeness. In what sense was that time God's ideal moment?

Jesus did not come sooner because the world was not ready, and He did not come later because the ideal moment would have been past. Three mighty forces were at work, converging on this time and the certain place God had chosen. In the order of their value in an ascending scale, they were the Roman, the Greek and the Hebrew forces. These forces met with their contributions at Christ's birth, and they met again at His death, dramatized in the inscription which Pilate had written above His cross – in Latin, Greek and Hebrew.

A. The conquest of the world by Rome—the *material* contribution

The first force that was used to create God's ideal moment was the *conquest of the world by Rome*. It was a Roman world into which Jesus was born. Two contributions of Rome were apparent in God's preparation of the world when "the time" came.

One was the Roman *roads*. When Rome conquered a province, she immediately built a road to that new colony—a very substantial road. Those same road settings exist to this day, and I have traveled several of them! I have even seen (and stepped on) the ruins of some of the original roads! These roads provided arteries of travel for the first Christian witnesses. These roads were to be the highway for the missionaries of the new Christian message and movement.

The other Roman contribution was Roman *rule*. Rome became master of the land and mistress of the sea over the entire known world of that day. The earth shook with the constant tramp of the feet of Rome's soldiers. Roman ships asserted authority over the known seas of that world.

Rome's entire history is a tale of warfare and conquest. But with each conquest she was bringing the entire world nearer a unity than it had ever known. Two hundred years before Christ was born, the conquest began with Rome conquering her entire homeland. Then the empire was spread to north Africa through the destruction of Carthage. Then Macedonia, Corinth, and soon all of Greece fell to Rome. Soon all of Asia Minor had been subdued, then Gaul and northern Europe. When Caesar Augustus returned from the battle of Actium, warmongering stopped – and the Prince of Peace was approaching! No hostile borders remained throughout the empire. Roman prowess had emptied the seas of pirates. Merchants and citizens of all classes could travel over the far-reaching Roman roads from one end of the empire to the other. It was a vast empire. The Apostle Paul boasted that he was a citizen of it.

One of the facets of Roman rule was that peace (the famous "Pax Romana") prevailed literally throughout the empire. The entire world was ready now for Christ and His Apostles, for Paul and the early Christian missionaries. They would be able to travel and minister freely without the impediment of local and national hostilities in the world. This peace was the product of Roman rule. The extension of Christianity could not have been brought about in so brief a time had it not been for the contributions of Rome.

In a final miraculous dovetailing of events, "there went out a decree from Caesar Augustus that all the (Roman) world should be enrolled" (for taxation). In Palestine "every one went into his own city. Joseph went up from Galilee into the city of David, which is called Bethlehem." What a marvel! God maneuvered a pagan Emperor's decree to fulfil Divine prophecy! These historical progressions were all part of Rome's contribution to "the fullness of the time."

B. The culture of Greece—the *mental* contribution

The second force that was sovereignly used to create God's ideal moment was the *culture of Greece.* While Rome conquered Greece by military power, Greece conquered Rome by mental power. Rome conquered by *clout*, Greece conquered by *culture*. Rome built its own material highways, while Greece built its own mental highways. One was as vital and necessary as the other.

When Jesus came, Greek culture was at its highest. No nation can conjure as famous a cultural heritage as ancient Greece. Listen to the lineup of elite contributors: Homer the poet; Herodotus, the historian; Solon, the wise lawgiver; Plato, the philosopher (whom one historian described as a "pre-Christian Christian," surely too bold, but a good indication of Plato's insights); Phidias, the sculptor; and Demosthenes, the orator. Alexander the Greek world-conqueror defeated the

Persian commander Darius on the plains of Arbela, and thriving Greek colonies sprang up almost immediately in the wake of his conquest. But Alexander's greatest achievement was not in his conquests; it was he who installed the rich Greek language into the known world of his day. The Greek language became so wide-spread that it came to be known in history as *Koine* ("common", the word from which the word, *koinonia*, comes, from which we in turn derive our word "fellowship") Greek. It was carried everywhere so that it became the universal language of that day.

To tie things together, let us be reminded that Jesus had a disciple named Philip, a Greek name derived from the Greek word, "philos," a lover. When the scholarly Greeks came to Jerusalem during Passover week (a great "watershed" or "hallmark" episode in the ministry of Jesus, recorded in John 12), a short time before Christ's death, they sought out Philip and said, "Sir, we would like an introduction to Jesus." Philip was uncertain about Jesus and Gentiles, so he went to Andrew, another disciple with a Greek name, and they together delivered the Greek seekers to Jesus.

It is evident that our Lord's preferred language was his native Aramaic, but it is very likely that He also had a command of the Greek language as well. His hometown of Nazareth as well as His later headquarters at Capernaum were on the great trade route from the Mediterranean to Damascus, and all the traders and travelers spoke Greek.

A universal language was needed as a common carrier of the glorious Gospel of the Son of God. We cannot today estimate how important the Greek language was for the propagation of early Christianity. The Old Testament which the Jews used in their synagogue worship outside of Palestine was the "Septuagint," a Greek translation. Paul, the "traveler and Roman citizen" (the title of Sir William Ramsey's book about Paul), went through Italy, Syria, Achaia, Cilicia and Macedonia speaking the Greek language, and men understood him everywhere. Our New Testament of today was written in this same Greek language, one of the most expansive and expressive communicating tools man has ever known.

With Grecian speech went Grecian thought. The old Greek philosophers, like Socrates, groped publicly after God and immortality, but were never satisfied with the offerings of Greek philosophy and thought. So God used pagan highways and a universal pagan peace as well as a pagan language to prepare the way for the coming of the Lord.

C. The civilization of the Hebrews – the *moral* contribution

The final force that was sovereignly used to create God's ideal moment was the moral *civilization* of Israel. Just as "three (a merely traditional number) wise men" have been imagined as coming to the birth of Jesus, three great civilizations converged in "the fullness of the time," and each brought its "gift" for the coming of Christ.

Of the three great contributions (the Roman, the Greek and the Hebrew), the contribution of the Hebrew religion was the greatest. The God of Israel was the God of the Messiah, the "God and Father of our Lord Jesus Christ"! The Jews were His "chosen people" – chosen by Jehovah God to perpetuate and to propagate the worship of the one true God. Their God was a living God, standing in vital contrast to those made of wood, stone, silver or gold. Furthermore, unlike the pagan and heathen gods around them, their God was a God of purity, not impurity. Their faith was marked by a high morality.

From the very beginning, Israel was preparing the way for the Messiah who was coming. He was the theme of the Psalmist, the prediction of every prophet, and the hope of every Jewish mother. The blood sacrifices that were commonly made on Hebrew altars were types of the coming Redeemer from sin. Every patriarch, every judge, every king, every priest, every prophet, was a herald, telling of the One who was coming.

The Hebrew Scriptures from Genesis to Malachi was marked with the foot-prints of the coming Messiah. Through the history of the Jews the living God moved to the climax of the far-reaching event, the coming of His Son, Emmanuel, "God with us," God manifest in the flesh. In their literature He had been foretold to Adam as a man; to Abraham as to his nation; to Jacob as to His tribe; to Isaiah as to His family; to Daniel as to His time; to Jeremiah as the seed of David; to Micah as to the town of His birth; to Haggai as to His coming into the Temple; to Mary as to His person; by a star as to the exact house of His birth. The last of the prophets, John the Baptist, fulfills his prophetic calling by speaking the sentence he was born to declare, "Behold, the Lamb of God, who takes away the sin of the world!" Someone said, "With that announcement, prophecy was closed, and history began." The fullness of *the time* had come.

It was the Sunday of the Christmas pageant in December of 1979. The entire cast of the pageant was getting ready with last-second preparations. I was standing on the sidewalk at the main entrance door, welcoming people as they entered the church. An automobile came hurrying up to the curb and the door opened quickly. A young woman stepped out, carrying her baby, who was to play the role of the Baby Jesus in the Christmas pageant which was scheduled to begin in just a few minutes. As she hurried from the car, the mother said abruptly, "*Excuse* us; Baby Jesus is *late!*" I thought to myself, "*Not really! That's one thing Baby Jesus was not, and would never be – late!*" It was in the fullness of time that He came, God's ideal moment.

II. It is the Story of God's Ideal MAN, 4b

Second, the salvation story concerns God's ideal *Man*. "When the fullness of the time was come, *God sent forth His Son.*" The two most common summary statements in the New Testament of the Incarnation of God in human flesh are, "God gave His Son," and "God sent His Son." These sound similar, but the emphasis is on a technical difference in the two phrases.

"God gave His Son" emphasizes the love of God and the sacrifice of God in His gift. D. L. Moody, the great evangelist of nineteenth century America, once said, "Before I became a father, I preached a great deal about the sacrifice of Jesus the Son, but after I became a father myself, I preached less on the sacrifice of Jesus the Son and more on the sacrifice of God the Father." John 3:16 suggests that when it reminds us that "God so loved the world that He gave His only begotten Son."

The other phrase, "God sent forth His Son," is quite different in its emphasis. We never speak accurately today of a typical baby being "sent forth." Today's baby is "conceived," "formed," and "born," but not "sent forth." The term "sent forth" suggests that Jesus had already pre-existed somewhere else before He came to the earth, and that is true. Everybody else had a beginning of existence when he or she was conceived and born, but not Jesus. He is unique in that His life did not begin with His human conception or birth. He had a "pre-Bethlehem" existence, indeed, for all eternity.

The term, "His Son," reveals the Deity of the Son of God. He did not *become* the Son of God when He was conceived and born – or at His baptism, death or resurrection. He always *was* the Son of God from eternity past. He was the eternal Son of God, as God the Father is the eternal Father. Note, also, the support that this phrase gives to the doctrine of the Trinity. God the Father and God the Son are two distinct Persons, or the One could not send the Other. As a distinct Person within the Godhead, Jesus was co-existent, co-eternal, and co-equal with the Father (and the Holy Spirit) from all eternity.

One commentator said of this phrase, "The terms used here require to be very closely considered: they are fraught with the very essence of the Gospel." The term translated "sent forth" adds other dimensions to the story. The word is *exapesteilin*, a triple compound word in the Greek language. This compound verb occurs in nine other places in the New Testament, all of them in Luke's Gospel and the Book of Acts. In every case, the idea is stressed that the person sent belonged intimately to the place or the society of the person who sent him. In verse four, as well as verse six, there is the thought of heaven as the sphere of existence from which the Son and the Spirit were sent.

Exapesteilin is a big word comprised of three smaller words. The root word means "to send." The second preposition in this compound word is "apo," which means "away from." And the first preposition is "ex," which means "out," or "out of." The two prepositions suggest separation or severance, and the suggestion is that the coming of Jesus to the earth meant pain and deprivation for the Sending One. God sent forth away from Himself, that is, out of His immediate Presence, His own Son – and it involved pain. Paul stressed this truth in Romans 8:32 when he said, "*God spared not even His own Son, but delivered Him up for us all.*" All of us have considered the pain of Jesus on the cross, but what about the suffering of God the Father?

The word "sent" is an aorist tense verb, describing an act that occurred only one time. This word is used by Jesus over forty times in the Gospel of John alone to describe the Father's action in His Incarnation. "God sent forth His Son." He is God's ideal Man.

III. It is the Story of God's Ideal METHOD, 4:4c

Third, the salvation story concerns God's ideal *method*. "God sent forth His Son, *made (born) of a woman.*"

Again, the phrase is replete with meaning. The very language, "made of a woman," implies the possession of a higher nature. If the Son possessed only humanity, why would it be necessary to say that he was "made of a woman"? *That* is obviously true of every other person, but here there is a distinction. The specific phrase points significantly to His supernatural human conception, for there is a conspicuous exclusion of human fatherhood. The obvious suggestion of the phrase is that Jesus was born *only* "of a woman," without the biological agency of human fatherhood. Whether Paul intended it or not, this phrase is totally consistent with the Biblical teaching of the virgin birth of Christ.

The phrase also points out His real and true humanity. How crucial this is! Without His sharing in our humanity (Hebrews 2:14), He could not possess either the natural or legal union with us, both of which are necessary for Him to accomplish all of the work He performed for our salvation. Being "made of a woman," He took upon Himself all human experiences, shared our emotions, wept our tears, partook of our joys, hoped and feared as we do, grew as we grow, and in everything but sin, was a man among men. It is His humanity that enables Him to be "the Second (true and representative) Man," and "the Last Adam," but that is too great a subject for this brief study.

There are four distinct births mentioned in the context of our passage in Galatians four. One is the birth of *Ishmael*, who was begotten of the flesh (verses 22 and 23). A second is the birth of *Isaac*, who was begotten as the child of promise (verses 22 and 23). Another is the birth of *Jesus*, who was born of a woman without the agency of a male (suggested in verse 4). The fourth birth is the new birth of *the child of God*, who is spiritually born of the Spirit of God (suggested in verse 6). A word of caution is necessary with regard to this last-named birth. To say a birth is spiritual does not in any way detract from its reality. My spiritual birth is as real and as revolutionary as was my physical birth. Just as a new being was brought into existence by my physical birth, an entirely new being was brought into existence by my spiritual birth. Just as all human possibilities are potential through human birth, all spiritual possibilities as a child of God become potential at the moment of spiritual birth.

A young man, trying to explain his wife's inability to have children, said, "My wife is impregnable." Realizing that didn't sound quite right, he tried to correct it by saying, "No, she is inconceivable." Realizing he had gone from bad to worse, he made a final effort. "I guess you could just say she is unbearable." No matter how inadequate his explanation, she still couldn't have children! No matter how inadequate our explanation, Jesus was still virgin-born! Thus His humanity was protected from original sin.

There are also four distinct ways in which human beings have come into existence. These are: (1) By *direct creation* – that is, without a man or a woman, as Adam (this was not creation out of nothing, but out of dust); (2) By *Divine construction* – that is, through the removal of one from the other (construction from previously existing material), as Eve from Adam; (3) By *dynamic conception* – that is, through sexual union of man and woman, as all other mere mortals; (4) By *Divine conception* – that is, by birth from a woman, but without a man, as Jesus.

God engineered Adam out of dust. God engineered Eve out of Adam. God decreed the existence of Cain (and all other mere men) out of a union between man and woman (Adam and Eve). And God engineered Jesus out of Mary, without a man. Adam was *created* – without the instrumentality of either man or woman. Eve was *constructed* by God – using the instrumentality of an already-existing man, but even *then*, the *man* was not active in her construction (Eve was made by God out of Adam). Cain was *conceived*, with the joint instrumentality of a man and a woman. And Jesus was *conceived by God*, using only the instrumentality of a *woman*. Explaining the birth of Jesus, Matthew Henry said, "The God who took a motherless woman out of the side of a man to make Eve, took a fatherless man out of the body of a woman to produce Jesus." The phrase, "made of a woman," points out this uniqueness of Jesus. This was God's ideal Method.

IV. It is the Story of God's Ideal MODEL, 4d

Fourth, the salvation story concerns God's ideal *model*. "When the fullness of the time had come, God sent forth His Son, made of a woman, *made under the law."* The entire struggle of the surrounding context in Galatians three and four has to do with bondage to the law and freedom from the law. Jesus was born subject to the Levitical law as a Jew, to the social law (being subject to His parents, Luke 2:51), to the civil law (seen in His paying of taxes, Matthew 17:24-27), and to the moral law (He was perfect in following its precepts of morality). He also made Himself subject to the penalties of the law, though He was Himself sinless. He made Himself subject to the death which was the penalty of the broken law, though He never broke the law. It was by taking the death which the law mandated for us as sinners that He was able to save us. It was by this total obedience to the law that He triumphed over the law. The law exists for evil-doers; it is powerless against the good. Jesus took His place both by His Father's assignment and by His own willingness, in order that He might stand in as Surety for lawless sinners.

In Matthew eight, Jesus met a Roman centurion who had a great understanding of Him. Speaking to Jesus, the centurion said, in effect, "I understand You, because I also am a man under authority." This man understood authority since he submitted to it and exercised it. Jesus lived under "higher authority," the authority of the Lord and the authority of the law. Made under the law, He assumed all of the obligations of the law, lived a perfect meritorious obedience to the law, and made Himself liable to the claims the law had upon us. Jesus Christ has fulfilled all the claims of the law for us, both as to the precepts of the law and as to the penalty of the law. In a staggering verse, Galatians 3:13 says, "Christ has redeemed us from the curse of the law, being made a curse for us."

The fact that Jesus was "made under the law," and subject to the law, and fully compliant with the demands of the law, made Him God's ideal Model.

V. It is the Story of God's Ideal MOTIVE, 5

Fifth, the salvation story concerns God's *ideal motive.* "When the fullness of the time had come, God sent forth His Son, made of a woman, made under the law, to redeem them that were under the law, that we might receive the adoption of sons."

Two related purposes comprised God's motive in sending His Son. One was to "redeem" sinners. His object was to redeem both Jews and Gentiles from the *curse of the broken law,* and from *the slavish compulsions* of the law's demands. This He did by taking the penal consequences of sin, with its curse and wages (Galatians 3:13), upon Himself. Note the great thought that the deliverance He wrought for us was the result of an act of purchase. The word translated "redeem" means that Jesus has bought sinners altogether out of the slave market of sin and released them from their bondage to sin.

This He accomplished by His terrible death in behalf of sinners on the Cross.

Three great salvation words are used or suggested in these verses, the words "redemption," "regeneration" and "adoption." Jesus came and died to *redeem* us, the coming of the Spirit into our hearts effects our *regeneration* (our new birth), and we are simultaneously *adopted* into God's family.

The word, "adoption" (verse 5), introduces another gigantic concept into the story. "God sent forth His Son . . . to redeem . . . that we might receive the adoption of sons." This question must be asked: If I am *born* into God's family when I am saved (the new birth), then why must I also be *adopted?* Both birth and adoption will bring a person into a family; then why are they both necessary in the case of a Christian? Simply stated, the birth gives me my new *nature,* God's own nature, as a Christian. II Peter 1:4 says that the believer becomes "a partaker of God's nature." Adoption, on the other hand, gives me my *standing* in God's family. When I am born, I become a "child" (*tekna,* in Greek; the word for an infant who is not yet able to talk) in God's family. But when I am adopted, I become a "son" (*huios,* in Greek, one with full adult standing) in God's family. Let it register deeply in your heart: Jesus Christ became the son of man that we might become sons of God. He was "born of a woman" that we might "receive the adoption of sons." The word for "adoption" is *huiothesia,* which means "son-placing", or installation into the position of *a fully adult son with privileges and resources that match this position.* An heir cannot receive his inheritance as long as he is an under-age child, but a fully mature son is entitled to his total inheritance.

So adoption is crucial to let the Christian know that he has full privileges, full resources and *full responsibility* when he is saved.

So God's motive in saving sinners is to remove them from the bondage of sin and give them His great freedom, and to give them full privileges, resources and responsibility in His family. This is God's ideal motive.

It seems to be Paul's intention in the successive phrases of this text to mark the successive steps which the Son of God followed in His pursuit of our redemption. The first step is that He was "*sent forth*" from the bosom of the Father; the second step, He was *made the son of a woman*; then, He was *brought under the law*; and finally, in the word "*redeemed*" He bought out from under the law's jurisdiction and penalty all those who are born of the Spirit. The latter, of course, *includes His crucifixion* as the means of redemption. So four distinct steps can be traced here in His saving work for us.

A final practical idea should be carefully noted here before we consider the final point of the message. The word "redeem" means "to free a person from bondage or captivity by paying a price." Note that the person is not redeemed unless he is freed. A redemption which leaves the bound person in captivity is a contradiction in terms. It is unthinkable that a ransom be paid and the person still remain a prisoner. If you profess that you have been redeemed, are you living in the freedom of Christ? Are you celebrating that freedom? Is your life a credit to Christ, even with all the struggles against the flesh that are common to such a life? Is God's ideal Motive being fulfilled in your life?

VI. It is the Story of God's Ideal MIRACLE, vs 6

Finally, the salvation story concerns God's ideal *miracle*. "And because ye are sons, God hath sent forth the Spirit of His Son into your hearts, crying, Abba, Father." This is the second

The Salvation Story

occurrence of the term, "sent forth," in the passage. In the first (verse 4), God sent forth His Son into the world; in the second (verse 6), God sent forth His Spirit into our hearts. The first is the objective foundation for the salvation of sinners; the second is the subjective experience that makes that salvation personal. Romans 8:9 says, "If any man hath not the Spirit of Christ, he is none of his." This may mean that Christ does not belong to him, or it may mean that he does not belong to Christ. Both are true if the Holy Spirit is not in an individual—he doesn't belong to Christ, and Christ does not belong to Him.

Our entire salvation depends upon the incoming and indwelling Person of the Holy Spirit. It is the Spirit who convicts us to prepare us for His incoming. It is the Spirit who converts us by His incoming. It is the Spirit who regenerates our previously dead spirit as He comes into us. It is the Holy Spirit who mediates the Presence of Christ within us, making Jesus very real to us. It is the Holy Spirit who "seals us unto the day of redemption," and gives us "the earnest" (the down payment) which is the first "payment" of all benefits we possess in Christ.

Here, the Presence of the Holy Spirit in our hearts has a special meaning and purpose. That special meaning is suggested in a similar passage in Romans 8:15, which says to believers, "Ye have received the Spirit of adoption, whereby we cry, Abba, Father." The similarity between the two passages is evident. In both passages, the Holy Spirit is identified as the Spirit of adoption, an identification that deserves a world of interpretation and explanation. In both passages, it is the Holy Spirit who stimulates the cry of our hearts, "Abba, Father." What a beautiful statement! The word "Abba" is the word for a father in the Aramaic language, and the word *pater*, translated "Father" in the text, is the same word in the Greek language. So here Jew and Gentile are united in

Christ. Here the experience of regeneration is seen to be commonly needed by all men. The word "Abba" is the tender word, often translated "Daddy" or "Papa." So it is the Holy Spirit who puts the most tender confidence of intimacy with God in a new believer's heart.

But there is far more in this passage. In Galatians 4:5, two purposes are given for the coming of Jesus into the world. The second purpose that "that we might receive the adoption of sons." Note carefully the union of the term "adoption" and "sons." The word adoption is the word for the full placing of a son in the status of adult privilege and responsibility. The word "sons" as distinct from the word "children" is the word which pictures full adult privileges in a family. The word "child" pictures an infant; indeed, the word contains the idea of an infant which is unable to talk yet. The word "son," on the other hand, is the word which means full status and privilege in responsible adulthood.

Take a few moments and re-read the entire passage (Galatians 4:1-7), noting the use of the word "heir" in verses 1 and 7. Note in verse 7 that the word "son," the word which denotes maturity instead of infancy, is associated with the word "heir" in verse 7. Note the emphasis on maturity of age as the qualification for receiving an inheritance to which you are entitled. In the passage, the world before the coming of Christ is like a child who may be entitled to the inheritance, but is not "of age." Then, "when the fullness of the time had come, God sent forth His Son." Now, the entire race of men has a right to the inheritance of God's sons. However, only those who are born again get the inheritance. And even those who are born again may not exploit all the riches to which they are entitled as sons of God. Dear Christian, are you leaving the riches to which you are entitled in Christ in the Bank? Are you exploiting your spiritual bank account for the advantage of Jesus and His purpose? Are you living below your privileges and possessions as the heir of God?

Several years ago, I read an article in the daily newspaper entitled, "States Hold Millions in Unclaimed Funds." The article contained these statements: "Millions of dollars worth of unclaimed bank accounts, stock dividends, utility deposits and insurance settlements sometimes languished untouched for years. Last year about $780.7 million in unclaimed money was collected by state governments, and this year the total could reach $1 billion. Only about 25% of the money turned over to state governments is ever returned to the owners or claimed by the heirs."

In a separate kind of case, one unprecedented in the annals of history in the United States, New York City Surrogate attorney William T. Collins "reluctantly" ruled that Eugene F. Suter, Jr., had a legal right to reject the $400,000 left him by the elder Suter, inventor of the permanent wave machine. The order legally cut off the 22-year-old Yale student from all future interest in the family fortune, leaving him without an income.

Collins' ruling sustained Suter's formal declaration of renunciation "for moral and political reasons," filed sometime earlier despite strong protests by trustees of his father's estate. Many people reading this account would wonder about the sanity of the young man in turning down such a large sum of money.

Do you see the similarities between the follies of allowing a fortune to which you are entitled to go unclaimed, or rejecting a fortune to which you are entitled? Yet the Word of God declares that both are possible in eternal matters. A Christian is entitled to a fabulous fortune of spiritual riches, but he may allow it to go unclaimed and unused by his unbelieving preoccupation with his own poor interests. And though the title deed has been purchased by the blood of Christ to make the inheritance of eternal life and all that is included available, you may still reject the inheritance. Eugene Suter's only explanation was, "I have two hands and a head of my own." And many reject salvation for the same reason. "I can take care of myself; I don't need anybody's help." Empire builder Ted Turner said, "I don't need somebody else's death for me. If Jesus Christ died for me, He shouldn't have bothered." The Apostle Peter described what Turner missed in these words, "An inheritance incorruptible, and undefiled, and that fades not away, reserved in heaven for you"—and that is only a part of the estate! What about you? If you are a Christian, are you daily "cashing checks" on your spiritual account for the advance of Christ's cause? If you are not a Christian, repent of your sins and receive Jesus Christ into your heart today, totally trusting Him and Him alone to save you, and you will instantly become an heir of God and a co-heir with Jesus Christ.

Some three years ago, I was privileged and blessed to read Frances Hodgson Burnett's <u>Little Lord Fauntleroy</u>, which is a remarkable story about a remarkable (almost angelic) young boy. It is a touching story of how a young American boy's life is turned upside down when he becomes the sole heir to a vast fortune in England. While Cedric Errol, the boy who is heir to the estate, is allowed to use some of his grandfather's wealth as he pleases in America, the full extent of his privileges as Lord Fauntleroy have to wait until he is living in England with his grandfather. While in America, though he is far richer than he was before he became aware of his full identity and inheritance, he still gets only a small taste of his grandfather's wealth, but in England, he will see exactly what it means to be Lord Fauntleroy. Even so, dear Christian, you are a member of heaven's nobility today, you have the title deed to a fortune today, and you may negotiate great riches by employing what Charles Spurgeon called "faith's checkbook" today, but you cannot possibly know what is held in store, "reserved in heaven," for all of God's sons and daughters. As Christians, we may just praise God moment-by-moment that we have been included in His vast plan, and that the dividends will never stop "accruing to our account." In heaven, we will fully see with undimmed eyes what it means to be children of God.